DOGS, BUMPS & BABIES

Preparing Your Dog For Life With Your Baby

Aileen Stevenson

Copyright © Aileen Stevenson, 2021

ISBN: 9798735200956

ABOUT THE AUTHOR

Aileen Stevenson is a dog trainer and behaviour consultant specialising in family dog training. She works with families to tackle the challenges that dogs and children inevitably bring and helps them build happy, harmonious and stress-free lives together. She is a Certified Training Partner of the prestigious Karen Pryor Academy for Animal Training and Behaviour, and a full member of the Institute of Modern Dog Trainers. In addition, Aileen is Scotland's first, and currently only, Family Paws Licensed Educator - professional trainers with specific specialist knowledge and training to support new and expectant families with dogs. Her advice on the subject of safely integrating kids and dogs has been featured on BBC Radio, The Chicago Times and various podcasts.

Aileen champions kind, ethical, positive reinforcement based training and is passionate about helping owners understand their dogs better.

A mum to two daughters, Aileen has juggled dogs and kids from both sides – introducing new babies to a resident family dog and introducing a new dog into a home with children. She knows first hand how much children benefit from growing up with a family dog and is passionate about teaching families how to understand and live happily with their dogs.

Previously an accountant for 26 years Aileen began studying training and behaviour in order to help her own reactive rescue dog, Charlie. Her interest in behaviour quickly snowballed and Aileen eventually left balance sheets for dog training and founded The Perfect Puppy Company.

Aileen lives in Glasgow with Charlie and her family.

VOCABULARY

In this book I use the word 'owner' to refer to the human caregiver of a dog. There are other words or phrases I could have used…caregiver, guardian, pet parent etc. I use owner because it flows better (for me) and I find the other phrases a little 'clunky'. The choice of word doesn't imply any rank or hierarchy. My dog is a hugely important member of my family and certainly not a good or chattel!

I use the masculine pronouns 'he' and 'his' in this book only because all my dogs have been boys and they are generally in my mind when I write!

CONTENTS

INTRODUCTION

Are you an expectant parent with a dog? Or are you an expectant and excited grandparent with a dog? If so, then this book is for you! It will give you the information you need to help you, and your dog, prepare for life as a family with children.

Who needs this book?

Every dog owner whose dog is going to be around babies or young children will benefit from reading this book. Every dog - regardless of breed, size, temperament or previous training - will benefit from some proactive planning to gently introduce the changes a new human pup brings.

The practical, simple information and advice contained here will enable you to get off to the best possible start as a family with dogs and children. It will help you lay a solid, safe foundation for a mutually rewarding life together.

Why do you need this book?

The arrival of a baby is a huge lifestyle change. In fact, it's probably one of the most significant life events that we will ever face. Our lives change overnight when our first child is born and we are suddenly faced with a whole array of new experiences and challenges. As humans we understand this and so we take steps to prepare ourselves for these challenges as best we can. We attend ante natal classes, we read parenting books, we join internet forums, we write birthing plans and spend hours researching products in minute detail. We do all these things because we understand that preparation in advance will help to make our lives easier when our baby arrives. Feeling prepared (or as prepared as we can be) and having a plan gives us the confidence to face the changes and challenges ahead. We don't wing it and hope for the best.

If our lives are about to change dramatically then it's inevitable that the dogs we share our lives with are also going to experience change and upheaval. Think of all the things that will potentially change for your dog with the arrival of a newborn. They're almost certainly going to receive less attention, exercise levels are likely to decrease, their access to certain areas of the home may be restricted, new rules may be put in place. Many aspects of their life are likely to change and if all these changes happen simultaneously and overnight then it's hardly surprising that some dogs may struggle with the transition from being a dog living with a couple to a family dog.

Often our attitude to our dogs themselves, and to their behaviour, changes with the arrival of our child. Behaviours which were tolerable or acceptable (or even enjoyable....your dog snuggling in bed with you, for example) are suddenly re-framed when there is a baby in the picture. From our dog's perspective nothing has changed but from ours everything has, and our tolerance of some behaviours suddenly changes too.

Sadly, pregnancy and the arrival of a new baby are two common reasons that dogs are surrendered by their owners for re-homing. The reasons new and expectant parents feel they have no option but to surrender their dogs are varied and range from behavioural problems to simply feeling that they no longer have sufficient time to devote to their dog. It's important to acknowledge that sometimes the decision to rehome is absolutely the right one. Not every dog can live safely and happily with young children and some dogs require more attention or care than new parents have to give. In those cases it's better for everyone – humans and dogs – to find a new, more suitable home for the dog. But in many, many cases some simple preparation and planning in advance could have made the transition from dog parents to parents with a dog less stressful and more successful.

How will this book help you?

This book takes a simple, practical approach to help you maximise your chances of success and reduce potential stress for you and your dog. You don't need to be an experienced dog trainer to put in place the advice given here, just a committed owner.

This book will help you consider –

- your dog's personality and how that might affect the way he reacts to your baby

- what elements of your dog's life might change and how we can make those changes easier?

- how to gently introduce the many new things that come with a new baby

- the things your dog already does that might be helpful when there's a baby in the home and how we can make those stronger

- the things your dog already does that might be unhelpful when there's a baby in the home and how we can teach him something better

- how to read your dog. Understanding when a dog is feeling stressed or worried is a key element in keeping children and dogs safe

- how to introduce your dog to your new baby (and whether that's a helpful way to think of it)

- practical steps to make your life in the early days of parenthood easier

When should you read this book?

Now! Trying to teach your dog new things or tackling behavioural problems are not things you want to be doing when you have a newborn baby to care for. Teaching your dog to sleep happily downstairs, alone when they have previously been used to sleeping in your room is not a job for a sleep deprived new parent!

Beginning to make small changes well in advance is one of the keys to success. The more time you have to introduce changes or teach new things the less stressful the process will be for both you and your dog. And if you do hit any obstacles or difficulties you will have more time to work through them.

Your new routine, new rules or new behaviours will be well established, well practiced and routine by the time baby arrives.

Too often people approach me to discuss preparing their dog for the arrival of their new baby when they are only a few weeks away from their due date. By then Mum is often very tired, uncomfortable which can make implementing changes more arduous and the time pressure also adds stress and urgency to the situation. Make things easy on yourself and start as soon as you possibly can.

Congratulations!

Congratulations on being a proactive, responsible dog owner who recognises that changes are coming for your dog and who wants to make those changes as easy and comfortable as possible for them. Putting in place the ideas contained in this book will decrease stress and increase success. So let's get started

CHAPTER 1

DOES MY DOG KNOW I'M PREGNANT?

"Does my dog know I'm pregnant?" is a question that many pregnant women have asked themselves. A quick internet search or a chat with friends will throw up many instances where parents to be are convinced that their dog knows that they are expecting a baby. But do they really? And does it really matter either way? It may seem like a frivolous question but having a clearer understanding of what our dogs are experiencing, and why they behave as they do, can help us to help them. It's common for owners to create a narrative around their dog's behaviour, for example, "he's being protective" or "he's clingy because he knows I'm pregnant", but in doing so we run the risk of misinterpreting their behaviour. If a dog's behaviour changes during pregnancy it can be tempting to conclude that it's because he knows that his owner is pregnant. But let's step back and consider what your dog really knows.

Your Dog's Superpower

Scent is your dog's superpower. We see the world; they smell it. The area of a dog's brain which is devoted to interpreting and decoding scent is, proportionately, forty times greater than that of a human brain. Human noses contain only a tiny fraction (around 2%) of the scent receptor cells of a dog. Further, dogs have an additional scent organ, the vomeronasal organ, located near the roof of the mouth, which is largely non-functional in humans. The vomeronasal organ enables them to detect pheromones secreted by other dogs which signal their readiness to mate or their state of health. It's almost impossible for us to truly conceive of the sophistication and sensitivity of a dog's olfactory system. Since we are visual creatures perhaps a visual analogy will help give us some inkling of the extent of dogs' sense of smell? Dr James Walker of Florida State University's Sensory Research Institute describes it thus, "...what you and I can see at a third of a mile, a dog could see more than 3,000 miles away...". Pretty staggering!

This amazing ability has been harnessed and utilised by humans in many ways. Most of us are familiar with the work of detection dogs who are trained to locate items like illegal drugs, explosives or other contraband items. The use of dogs to locate missing people in search and rescue operations is also well known. However, perhaps less familiar to many is the ability of dogs to detect physiological changes in humans. There are many reported cases of dogs showing intense interest in moles, skin lesions and specific areas of the body which, after investigation, were subsequently found to be cancerous. Medical detection dogs are trained to identify the scent of certain human diseases, like cancer, in samples of blood, urine or even breath. At the time of writing the world is in the midst of the COVID-19 pandemic and research is currently underway to determine whether dogs can be used to detect the presence of COVID-19 in samples of breath. Medical alert dogs are able to detect subtle changes in a person's odour which warn of an imminent health emergency like a seizure or a dangerous drop in blood sugar levels. So does this ability give us a clue about what our dogs might be experiencing?

It goes without saying that during pregnancy women experience dramatic physiological changes. Levels of hormones, particularly progesterone and oestrogen, increase dramatically and suddenly during pregnancy. In the course of one pregnancy a woman will produce more oestrogen that she would in an entire non-pregnant lifetime. In addition, new hormones specific to pregnancy are produced. Human Chorionic Gonadotrophin (hCG) is the hormone detected by pregnancy tests and is only produced during pregnancy. Interestingly male hormone levels also change during pregnancy! Yet more changes occur in hormone levels related to thyroid function, milk production, ligament relaxation and more. Last, but certainly not least, is the baby itself. If a dog can detect cancer cells in a blood sample or a minute drop in blood glucose levels it doesn't seem like a huge leap to suggest that a dog might be able to detect the scent of the baby itself. Given this superpower it is entirely reasonable to think that a dog living with a pregnant woman will be able to detect these significant physiological changes. There is no definitive evidence to date to prove this beyond doubt but there is also little to suggest that it's not possible.

You're Being Watched

What about changes other than scent? Anyone who lives with a dog knows just how closely they observe our body language and behaviour, and how attuned to their humans they can be. They notice, and attach meaning to, many things we do like switching off our computers or laying down our phones. These acts often signal interaction with our dogs and, as a result, they notice them.

Aside from changes which may be detected by scent there are many other behavioural changes which a pregnant woman may display. In the early stages of pregnancy they may be less active due to tiredness. Hormonal changes can make an expectant mum more emotional so she may cry more. Morning sickness may have them running to the bathroom. As pregnancy progresses a woman's gait changes as her centre of balance shifts and she may become more breathless and move more slowly as she becomes larger and heavier. Being such close observers of their humans' behaviour it seems likely that these changes don't go unnoticed by the dogs we share our lives so closely with. Could it even be possible for a dog to detect the sound of a foetal heartbeat? Some believe a dog's hearing is acute enough for that to be possible.

Knowing ≠ Understanding

All things considered, it seems certain that dogs can detect many changes which affect an expectant mum. But does it then follow that he knows you are pregnant or understands what that means?

No. Although your dog knows that something has changed he doesn't know what those changes predict.

For some dogs the changes that pregnancy brings, physiological and otherwise, can lead to changes in their own behaviour. They may sniff or lick mum more, may become clingy or protective of mum or show intense interest in her bump. They may display signs of anxiety or appear generally less settled. And, of course, they may not appear to notice any changes whatsoever and their behaviour may remain unchanged. Just like us our dogs are individuals and react to things in their own way.

Summary

In summary, given their amazing sensory abilities it seems very likely that dogs are aware of the many changes that pregnancy brings which can, for some dogs, lead to behavioural changes which suggest that "your dog knows you are pregnant'. However, as we have learned, although they know that changes are afoot they have no understanding of what those changes mean.

Key Points From This Chapter

- Your dog will be aware of physiological and behavioural changes

- Your dog doesn't understand what those changes mean

- Your dog's behaviour can be affected by the changes he detects

CHAPTER 2

WHO ARE YOU? THE IMPORTANCE OF KNOWING YOUR DOG

"Today you are you, that is truer than true. There is no one alive that is you-er than you"

Dr Seuss

There are nearly 8 billion people on this planet and they are all different. We can categorise all those people by race, nationality, religion, gender and myriad other ways but, no matter what boxes we put people in, one thing remains true. They are all – each and every one of them – individuals with their own likes and dislikes, hopes and fears, feelings and emotions.

The same is true for the dogs we share our lives with. Each one is an individual in their own right who experiences the world around them in their own unique way. Just as we like to categorise people and make assumptions about them based on those categories, we also make assumptions about dogs based on our own biases.

Those biases might be based on our own previous experiences, for example, do we assume that our existing dog will like a specific activity just because our previous dog did? Or do we control and curtail our existing dog's behaviour because of things a previous dog did? Our previous experiences with other dogs affect how we see the dog in front of us right now. Society also perpetuates a lot of perceived wisdom about what dogs "should" do or how dogs "should" behave. Dogs need walked at least twice a day. Dogs should sit to get a treat. Dogs should never growl. These statements are all examples of blanket statements which are applied to all dogs but which take no account of individual traits or preferences.

Perhaps the biggest way in which we categorise dogs is breed. How many times have you heard someone explain or excuse a dog's behaviour based on breed? Perhaps you've done it yourself? He's greedy because he's a Labrador. He's friendly because he's a Cockapoo. He barks because he's a Schnauzer. While there's no denying that breed traits exist (because we've deliberately selected for them over many generations) it's also true that variability exists as much within breeds as between them. Making assumptions about a dog's behaviour or preferences based solely on breed can blind us to their individuality.

Why is it important to really know, and understand, the individual dog in front of us?

The first step in working with your dog to help prepare them for the changes ahead is to pinpoint where your limited time, effort and resources are best spent. When you are expecting a baby you have lots of demands on your time – attending ante natal classes, reading baby books to prepare yourself, perhaps undertaking work in your home like decorating a nursery or finishing off any DIY jobs while you have the time (and energy!). In short, you have limited resources so you need to identify what key areas will have the greatest impact on reducing stress and increasing success for your dog....and remember, less stress for your dog means less stress for you.

If you clearly understand what is likely to be worrying or exciting for your dog, whether there are any key gaps in his training and whether there are any behavioural issues which need to be addressed you are well on your way to coming up with a practical plan which will make a real difference to your life as a family. The better you know your dog the more accurately you are likely to be able to predict his behaviour and the better placed you'll be to prevent problems arising.

The first step in the process is to ask yourself lots of questions about your dog's previous experiences, previous reactions to things, characteristics, likes, dislikes and more. Doing so gives you a jumping off point from which you can begin to home in on the things you'll need to work on.

Here's your first practical task. Listed below is a long list of questions about your dog. For a week or so pay close attention to your dog's behaviour in various different situations. Watch how he responds to different things in his environment – people, sounds, movement etc. Observe what he does when he's left to his own devices. Try to be as dispassionate and objective as you can; simply observe the behaviour without either judging it or excusing it.

Then, make yourself a cup of tea or coffee, grab a pad and a pen and start answering these questions. Be honest and objective. Note down the answer to each question (A/B/C) which you think best represents your dog and jot down any other thoughts or comments as you go. It can be helpful for each adult in the home to undertake this exercise separately and then compare notes. We all have individual relationships with our dogs and bring our own experiences to the table which means we all notice different things about our dogs. This will affect the answers we give to these questions. Some behaviours may be seen as more problematic by one partner than another and it is helpful to discuss these differences of experience and opinion. If you have more than one dog complete this exercise separately for each dog.

If there are any questions you aren't able to answer, for example, if your dog has never been exposed to children so you aren't sure how he would be likely to react, leave them for now. We'll come back to them...

Who Are You? Assessment Checklist

Socialisation

1. Describe your dog's previous behaviour around babies/young children.

   A   Relaxed, calm, either generally uninterested and/or able to interact calmly
   B   Excited, playful, enthusiastic
   C   Wary, hesitant, tense, barked or growled at the baby/child, avoided interaction OR highly excited, over aroused (jumping, barking, frantic

movement, straining to get to the baby / child

2. Describe your dog's previous behaviour around visitors to your home

    A   Relaxed, calm, either generally uninterested and/or able to interact calmly
    B   Excited, playful, enthusiastic
    C   Wary, hesitant, tense, barked or growled at the visitor, avoided interaction OR highly excited, over aroused (jumping, barking, frantic movement, straining to get to the person)

3. Describe your dog's behaviour towards strangers outside

    A   Relaxed, calm, either generally uninterested and/or able to interact calmly
    B   Generally good but he will occasionally pull towards people or jump up at them
    C   Lunges or barks at strangers outside OR highly excited, over aroused (jumping, barking, frantic movement, straining to get to the person)

4. Does your dog react to any specific groups of people? E.g. men, people in uniform, people carrying objects etc.

A No – generally calm and relaxed around people

B Occasionally – may sometimes bark/lunge at certain types of people/random people

C Yes – he regularly barks/lunges at people

Personality

5. How would you describe his normal energy levels?

A A bit of a couch potato – generally easy going with low energy levels. Happy with short walks and to snooze on the sofa the rest of the time

B Middle of the road – generally relaxed and settled if he gets a couple of good walks each day. Enjoys toys to entertain himself. Can be excitable or attention seeking if he doesn't get enough exercise

C Go, go, go! – Finds it hard to settle and relax at home. Needs regular long walks to burn off energy. Needs other activities at home to keep him engaged and occupied. Becomes frustrated or destructive without enough exercise.

6. How flexible in terms of routine is your dog?

   A   Very flexible and adaptable to changes in routines. Happy to have a lie in at the weekend!
   B   Will tolerate some changes in routine but will come looking for dinner or a walk after a while
   C   A creature of habit! He likes his dinner & exercise on the dot and will let you know if it's not!

7. How does your dog react to new things? For example, new pieces of furniture, objects moved from their usual place etc

   A   Inquisitive but relaxed; disinterested
   B   Initially wary and may take some time to approach the object but relaxes fairly quickly after they have investigated it
   C   Displays tense body language, will not approach the object, backs away from the object, remains suspicious for a longer time

8. How does your dog react to sudden/loud noises?

   A   Inquisitive but relaxed or disinterested; no response to the sound
   B   Acknowledges the sound; may startle but no strong fear response; recovers quickly

> C   Displays strong fear behaviours
> (panting, shaking, salivating, pacing,
> tries to hide or move away from the
> sound; takes a while to recover

9. How does your dog react to fast moving
objects?

> A   Inquisitive but relaxed; disinterested.
> No strong desire to chase
> B   May chase but can be successfully
> recalled
> C   Strong desire to chase. Unable to be
> recalled

10. How does your dog react to being handled?

> A   Relaxed body language. No areas of
> sensitivity
> B   Generally relaxed body language.
> May have certain areas where he is
> less keen than others to be touched.
> Moves away after a while.
> C   Tense body language. Resists being
> handled and would leave if given the
> choice. Particular sensitivity to
> having certain parts of their body
> touched

11. Does your dog ever guard objects or food?

> A   Never / Rarely
> B   Occasionally
> C   Regularly

12. Does your dog need to be physically close to you all the time?

    A   He likes to be close by but can happily settle in another room while I'm elsewhere in the home
    B   He will bark for a while if separated but can settle alone eventually
    C   He becomes destructive or distressed if he is not in close proximity to me

13. Does your dog bark or paw at you to initiate interaction?

    A   Never / Rarely
    B   Occasionally
    C   Regularly

14. How does your dog react to objects that move suddenly or unpredictably?

    A   Inquisitive but relaxed or disinterested; no strong response to the movement
    B   Acknowledges the movement; may startle but no strong fear response; recovers quickly
    C   Startles; tries to move away from the object; reluctant to approach

Training

15. Does your dog reliably do what you ask him
to?

    A Yes
    B Sometimes
    C Rarely

16. Does your dog walk calmly on a lead by your
side without pulling?

    A Yes – most of the time
    B Yes – until he gets distracted or
excited by something and then he
will pull
    C No – he often pulls

17. Does your dog jump up on you or on
strangers?

    A Rarely – he keeps his feet on the floor
most of the time
    B Sometimes – he will sometimes jump
up if excited
    C Yes – he jumps up a lot

18. Does your dog bark at the television, the
doorbell or at the sounds of people passing
by outside?

    A Never / Rarely

B   Occasionally; if he does it doesn't last
     for too long
C   Yes – he barks at the wind!

19. Will your dog go to his bed/mat/place if
    you ask him?

    A   Yes
    B   Sometimes
    C   Rarely

20. Can your dog respond to cues from a
    distance?

    A   Yes
    B   Sometimes
    C   Rarely

Once you and any other family members have
completed this exercise compare your answers. If
there are any questions you have answered
differently have a chat about why you have each
answered as you have and try to reach a consensus.

Are there any questions which you haven't been
able to answer? If so try to find a way to assess your
dog's behaviour under controlled conditions. For
example if your dog has never been around babies
or small children do you have any friends or family
with children that you could invite over in order to

observe your dog's behaviour? Or could you start walking him near a toddler's play park while you observe him closely to see whether he shows any interest in the children or any signs of anxiety? If you are exposing your dog to new things or taking them to an environment they have never been in before it's really important to make sure that your dog is comfortable at all times. Start at a distance and gradually move closer to the new thing paying close attention to your dog's body language at all times. If there is any suggestion of anxiety or worry then stop immediately and move away. Try to arrange multiple exposures to any new situations in order to get a true picture of how your dog behaves.

Once you have answered (and agreed on!) all the questions go back over your answers taking note of which answer you gave to each question – A, B or C. These will give you some indication of the areas where you should focus your attention and effort first.

Answer	Assessment
A	Minimal / little further training or preparation is indicated
B	Some further training or preparation is indicated
C	Significant further training or preparation is indicated

Now make a list, in descending order (C → A), of the issues described. You now have a clearer picture of which areas you, and your dog, will benefit from tackling most.

Summary

Taking the time to closely observe your dog's behaviour and think about their overall personality will give you an indication of the things that they may struggle with in relation to a new baby. It will also highlight any training gaps that might be more problematic with a baby in the picture. None of us have unlimited resources so knowing where to concentrate your efforts to make best use of those resources will help you plan effectively and efficiently.

In addition, identifying the areas where your dog is likely to cope well with minimal further training or preparation is reassuring and motivating. It allows you tick off those boxes and move on!

Key Points From This Chapter

- Understanding who your dog is will help you identify the areas that you need to focus on

- Be objective and honest in your answers

- Complete the exercise separately and then compare answers. Complete the exercise for each dog in your family

CHAPTER 3

ALL CHANGE!

"There is nothing permanent except change"

Heraclitus

Change is difficult. Think of the resolutions so many of us make each New Year. We decide to change our lifestyle for the better by going to the gym, or stopping smoking, or getting up earlier. We make grand plans that we believe will make a positive impact on our lives. We are motivated and know that these changes will change our lives for the better. These changes are our choice. And yet, more often than not, we fail.

We fail to successfully adapt to changes in our lifestyle that we chose to make, that we knew would benefit us and that we were motivated to achieve.

At the time of writing the world is in the midst of the COVID-19 pandemic. In our attempts to control the spread of the virus we have had significant changes imposed on our lifestyle. Our movements are restricted, our ability to socialise in a normal way with our friends and families is restricted, the way many of us work has changed significantly. These changes are all outwith our control and although we understand that they are for the safety and wellbeing of society as a whole most of us have struggled to adapt at some point.

Change is challenging. It's challenging when we are in control of that change and even more so when we are not.

It's no different for our dogs. Significant, sudden changes in their life can be stressful for them in just the same way as it is for us.

The arrival of a new baby is one of the most significant lifestyle changes we will experience in our lifetimes. A huge amount changes for us – not all of it easy. We sleep less, we see our friends less, our ability to socialise or take part in activities we enjoy like sport or exercise is likely to be less, we have less money, less time. For us, these changes are offset by the love that we feel for our baby and the joy at creating a family. Now imagine that all these changes were imposed on your life, with no warning and with no positive changes to counterbalance the negative ones. How would you feel? Confused? Frustrated? Stressed? Anxious?

It's a sad fact that the changes which affect our dogs' lives when a baby joins the family are often overlooked either because we simply don't give much thought to it or because we just assume that our dogs will adapt. And some of them will. Some will adapt to all these changes without any adverse impact on their behaviour at all. However, I think it's likely that some of these changes, particularly a decrease in attention and interaction, are nonetheless unpleasant or unsettling but some dogs can just 'suck it up' a bit better than others. Other dogs, however, will struggle with the impact of the changes suddenly affecting them and their stress or frustration can manifest as behaviours which are problematic for us – barking, destructive behaviour, looking for attention etc. Which is stressful for them and stressful for us.

Whether your dog is a long suffering stoic or a more sensitive personality we can go a long way to making the process of adapting to life with a baby less stressful by considering, in advance, what might change and how we can introduce those changes gently and gradually. This gradual approach means that your dog has the time to adapt to and get used to his 'new normal' by the time the baby arrives.

So, where to begin? Listed below are things which are likely to change for most dogs when a baby joins the family. This isn't an exhaustive list - not all of these will apply to every dog and there may be specific things not listed here that will apply to your dog. Use this as a jumping off point to get you started and feel free to add to it to make it relevant to you and your dog.

Routine

The early days with a new baby can be….chaotic! Feeding on demand, trying to snatch naps to catch up on precious sleep when you can, mountains of laundry to do and nappies constantly needing changed. A predictable routine often seems like an unattainable dream! Caring for our new baby is our priority and so it's inevitable that this will have a knock-on effect on our dog's routine. They may no longer always get their dinner at 6pm or be taken for a walk first thing in the morning.

For some dogs this may not be a problem. Think back to your assessment of your dog – are they a 'go with the flow' kind of dog who is flexible and will happily sleep through dinner time if you are late? Or are they a stickler for punctuality who will be expecting their dinner at a given time and complain if it doesn't appear?

If your dog lives by a reasonably rigid routine which

isn't subject to much change then begin to build some flexibility into their routine now. Start varying mealtimes a little each day. If meals always appear on the dot of 5pm then start serving it anytime between 4.50pm and 5.10pm, then 4.45pm and 5.15pm. Vary the times gradually aiming to build up to having a 1 hour window within which your dog is fed. One note here – while I'd still build some flexibility into breakfast times I'd always recommend feeding your dog his breakfast and letting him out to toilet as close to the start of your day as you can. In my experience he is far more likely to settle and let you get on with the other things you need to do than if you try to do those other things first while he waits to eat and toilet.

Do the same for exercise times and any other activities in your dog's day that have been ruled by the clock up until now.

Although our aim is to introduce a degree of flexibility into your dog's life it's also essential that some overall consistency and predictability remain. In order to feel secure and in control of our lives we benefit from a predictable framework within which to live and our dogs are no different. There may be variability in the detail but the big picture remains broadly predictable. It's a balancing act. Remember we're not aiming for pandemonium – just some pliability.

Exercise

Before my first daughter was born I had an office job. I would come home from work at around 6.30 and take my dog, Sydney, for a long walk to decompress from the day and blow away the cobwebs. We're fortunate enough to live on the edge of a village with direct access to riverbanks, woodland and grassland and Syd and I would walk there together. He was almost always off lead and we would often walk for miles through the woodland.

Then my daughter was born and all that changed pretty much overnight because I didn't know then all the things I know now. Suddenly his walks went from long, off lead walks through the fields to shorter walks on lead, around the streets while I pushed a pram. (As an aside…my original plans had been to continue to walk Syd off lead through the fields while I 'wore' my daughter in a baby carrier. However, she was born prematurely and was too small to be secure in the baby carrier. So my plans had to change. It's always worth considering that things may not always turn out as you hope and preparing for other eventualities is never a waste of time.)

Let's consider some of the ways in which your dog's

exercise might change.

Frequency & Duration

In the first whirlwind weeks of a baby's life, at least, many dogs will experience a decrease in the exercise they get both in terms of the frequency of walks and their duration. Early days with a newborn can be chaotic as you get to grips with being a parent and finding your rhythm and it's not unusual to find yourselves still in your pyjamas at lunchtime. On these days your dog may have to settle for a sniff in the garden, or a quick walk around the block, in place of his usual walk. The amount of free time we have also drastically reduces and you may simply not have time between feeds and nappy changes to go for long walks with your dog.

It's also worth considering that, post-birth, you may be less physically able to undertake the same amount of exercise you did previously. The type of birth you have, how well you recover from it and how tired you may feel after it are all unknown factors that will impact on your ability to exercise your dog.

Couples often say to me that they aren't too concerned about the dog getting less exercise as dad, or another partner, will walk the dog while mum stays at home with the baby. I normally caution against relying on that too much as I think, for first time parents, it can be hard to fully comprehend just how all-consuming it can be caring for a new baby and learning how to be a parent (which is, after all, what you will be doing). Dads/partners often find themselves just as immersed in caring for their child as mum does and often, at the same time, supporting mum. My advice would be always to work on the assumption that there will be a decrease in the amount of exercise your dog gets and plan for that. If things turn out differently that's great! But at least you're prepared.

Six to eight weeks before your baby's due date start to decrease the amount of exercise your dog gets slightly. Remember, we're aiming for gradual change that your dog can adjust to easily. If you usually go out for an hour reduce the duration to 50 minutes, then 45 minutes etc. You don't need to do this for every single walk but you want to create a gradual downward trend in the overall minutes of exercise your dog generally gets in a day. You should also start to replace one of their shorter walks with a snuffle and a play in the garden, or a just a short walk around the block. Again, you don't need to do this every day but start to build variability of both frequency and duration into your dog's routine. If you are decreasing physical exercise it's always a good idea to introduce some additional enrichment activities to give your dog something constructive to do. We'll cover that in more detail in a later chapter.

A word of warning! It can be tempting to think that if your dog is going to get less exercise then the exercise that they do get should be full of high energy, physically tiring activity like chasing a ball etc. No! Taking your dog to the park and using the ball chucker for half an hour of relentless chasing is likely to create a wired, over adrenalised dog who will then struggle to settle back home. Which is exactly what we don't want! After exercise our dogs should be calm, relaxed and ready to settle down for a sleep when they get home. A walk which includes the chance to run and play (if that's your dog's thing) and also includes slow, sniffy, low arousal activities is far more likely to result in a relaxed dog than a full on, frantic, high energy trip to the park.

Alongside a planned reduction in exercise we also want to encourage your dog to settle more. It sounds obvious but make sure they have access to a comfy bed in a cosy, quiet spot; some good chews to gnaw on....make it more likely that they will settle by giving them a comfortable place to do so.

Location

As I mentioned earlier in this chapter the locations where Syd was regularly walked changed overnight when my daughter was born. From woodland and riverbanks he was now more likely to be walked around the streets where I could easily and safely push a pram. That was almost certainly less interesting and enriching for him than what he had previously been used to.

Are the locations where you currently exercise your dog suitable terrain for a pram or a person wearing a baby in a sling? If the type of location or landscape where you exercise your dog is likely to change start adding in a few walks there in the weeks running up to your baby's birth. Or use the time now to scout out new locations that might be a good compromise for you both. For example, a park with level paved paths where you can push a pram but which also has open spaces or woodland where your dog can run and explore.

People

Will the person who normally walks your dog change? If mum-to-be is currently the person who most regularly walks the dog that will almost certainly change once the baby is born and mum is either recovering from the birth or simply has less time. So let's start to build that change into your dog's routine now. Some dogs are 'one person' dogs and may struggle to adapt to being walked by another person. Some dogs are more likely to listen to one owner over another and it will take time to build a bond and connection with someone. My own dog, Charlie, is very much <u>my</u> dog. He can be an anxious boy under some circumstances and he will sometimes refuse to go for a walk with other family members when he would more happily go with me. Whether or not your dog is anxious begin to mix up who is at the human end of the lead. If your dog needs to build a stronger connection outdoors with another family member, or a friend, if you are going to have friends helping you out in the early days, then it's best to start now. It helps the human too since they will also have learning to do about the dog – how well the dog responds to them, how good their recall is, how they react to different things outdoors etc. If there are any issues that arise – perhaps your dog is hesitant to go out with a new person or you discover that they don't respond to cues from their new walker – then you will have time to address these while you have the patience, energy and time to do so. Just a few walks each week with a different person, or people, is another small change which we can make in advance to make everyone's life easier.

Do you currently use a dog walker or a dog daycare for your pup? If so, I would strongly advise you to keep that on, even if you are going to be at home on maternity/paternity leave for some time. Knowing that your dog is being well exercised by someone you trust can be a huge weight off your shoulders during the early days of parenthood. It can help in so many ways – if your dog is getting less exercise from you (and as we've already discussed that's highly likely in most cases) then knowing he is getting a good run or walk once or twice a week takes away some of the guilt many new parents feel that the dog is being neglected. It maintains an element of constancy and predictable structure in your dog's life which is really important at a time of significant change. And it gives you the luxury of a few hours of dog free time each week which can be much needed and very restful. The responsibility of constantly meeting everyone's needs, and appropriately supervising can weigh heavily, especially if we are tired ourselves and a few hours of respite can help enormously to cope with that.

On Lead or Off Lead?

If your dog is currently walked off lead most of the time another point worth thinking about in advance is whether that is likely to continue. As I mentioned earlier my old boy, Syd went from the majority of his exercise being off lead to a significant portion of it being on lead after my first daughter was born. He didn't show any sign of struggling with that but, nonetheless, I could probably have made the change less stark for him if I'd introduced some on lead walks in advance. For me this change didn't cause any real issues (apart from also finding the walks around the neighbourhood less interesting and enjoyable than being in nature) for one major reason. Sydney walked well on a lead and didn't pull. Had he been a puller then walking him would have been a major difficulty. We're going to discuss problem behaviours in a later chapter but for now just consider whether the amount of time on lead is likely to increase for your dog and, if so, start to introduce a bit more on lead exercise now. Not only will it help your dog become accustomed to another small change in advance but, again it will highlight to you whether there are training issues you need to work on before your baby arrives.

Another common, but easily overlooked, problem I have come across in the past relates to the type of lead a dog is walked on. Many owners use extending, retractable leads to walk their dogs. As a trainer I'm not a fan of these leads for lots of reasons but it's undeniable that they are used by many people. At first glance there's no obvious issue but ask yourself how you will be able to push a pram while also holding a retractable lead? The design of these leads means that they have to be held in your fist which only leaves one hand free to push the pram. Which doesn't really work! To safely manoeuvre a pram you need both hands which is likely to mean that you'll need to change to a traditional lead which you can more easily hold whilst pushing your pram. If your dog has to learn to move with you without pulling on a fixed length lead rather than having the freedom of movement of an extendable lead now is the time to teach them.

Attention Levels

For many couples their dog has been their first 'baby'. Showered with love and attention they have had the luxury of lots of interaction with their humans. Inevitably having a baby means that you will have less time to devote to your dog. Your dog may have been used to always snuggling up beside you on the sofa or lying in your lap and that will not always be safe or appropriate if you are holding a baby in your arms. Both the attention you can give them and the proximity they can have to you (in some circumstances) will lessen. That can be a really hard adjustment for both you and your dog. Parents often feel very guilty that they can't devote the same time as before to their much loved dog. And the dog doesn't understand why things have suddenly changed.

So, how do we reduce the amount of attention and interaction we give our dogs without feelings of guilt or confusion? I like to reframe this for parents-to-be by saying that we're not removing attention, we're giving the dog fun things to do independently. Viewing things that way can help us see that this can be a positive change for our dogs. Giving them something enjoyable and enriching to do sounds a lot better than 'reducing attention', doesn't it?

At times when your dog may expect interaction with you, or close proximity to you, begin to offer them something like a tasty chew or a stuffed KONG ™ in their bed instead. Rather than just withdrawing attention and expecting our dogs to cope with that we are offering them an enjoyable alternative activity. In addition, these are low arousal occupations which will keep your dog absorbed for a time and will also generally encourage more settled behaviours.

Giving your dog fun, enriching activities which they can do independently of you helps them learn that they don't need all of your attention all of the time.

Sleeping Location

Does your dog sleep, unrestricted, in your bedroom with you? If not then feel free to ignore this section – you already have this box ticked!

If your dog does sleep in your bedroom with you, either on the bed itself or on the floor, then that will need to change. There are few absolutes in this book – not everything will apply to every dog in every family – but the rules around supervision are fundamental to keeping babies safe around dogs. Every dog has the potential to harm, albeit unintentionally in many cases, and the bottom line is if you aren't awake you can't supervise. Which means that a free roaming dog in your bedroom when you have an infant in the room is unsafe. If a dog is on the bed he could roll over and scratch the baby or cause a crushing injury. If the baby startles or cries out suddenly that may cause your dog to jump or startle himself. A baby stirring in the night in a crib by your bed or in your own bed may be enough to pique the interest of your dog and lead them to jump at the crib or bed. All of which leads us to the fact that if your dog sleeps in your room with you will have to introduce some changes to ensure the safety of your baby.

So what are your options? If you either want to have your dog close to you or must have them nearby as a necessity, perhaps because they suffer from separation related problems, then a crate is a safe option. If your dog is already crate trained then reintroduce it well in advance of your baby's due date to ensure that your dog is truly relaxed and happy sleeping there and it is totally normal to him by then. A pen may also be an option if you have a dog small enough to ensure that they are unable to jump out of it or push it over.

One thing to consider though is that, in the early days of parenthood at least, you will be up and down throughout the night feeding and changing your baby. Will this disturb your dog? Will they want to interact with you if you are up and about? Will they struggle to settle back to sleep if woken? If the answer to these questions is 'yes' you should consider whether being with you in your bedroom is really the best option for you and your dog.

My preferred option would be to teach your dog to sleep separately from you. It is the best option for everyone – dog and human - to get a decent night's sleep. If your dog has always slept in close proximity to you this is a big change for them. If they've been used to sleeping on your bed most of their life and suddenly find themselves in a different room, on their own, don't be surprised if they react by being unable to settle, barking or scratching at the door. This is one change that I would advocate starting to make as soon as you possibly can. It might take you a few nights of disrupted sleep if your dog struggles to settle away from you and needs reassurance so the time to start work on this is now, while you have the time, energy and patience to tackle it. You are sleep deprived enough as a new parent so that is not the right time to be dealing with a dog who is unsettled at night.

Firstly, think about where you would ultimately like your dog to sleep. Downstairs in the living room? On the landing? In a spare room? Make that place an appealing place to be – warm, cosy and with a comfortable bed suitable for the way your dog sleeps. If your dog sleeps curled up into a tight ball he may like a round bed with higher sides to snuggle into. If he sleeps stretched out then a larger, flatter bed will be more comfortable for him. How you introduce that new sleeping spot will depend on who your dog is and how he is likely to react to the change. Think back to the assessment of your dog's personality which you completed in chapter two. If your dog is a generally robust, confident dog who is able to settle alone at other times then you could simply try to introduce the new sleeping spot directly. Ask him to go to bed in his new spot (we'll cover how to train simple behaviours in chapter five) then calmly and quietly leave the room. You may find that he settles well. If so…awesome! If he is a little unsettled then some gentle reassurance may help. Don't leave him to bark it out…that's just stressful for him and for you. If you find he is not settling then adapt your plan and make the change more gradual. One way to do this is to move the bed further away from you in stages. Start with your dog's bed next to yours then gradually move the bed further across the bedroom from you, then out onto the landing, then to the bottom of the stairs etc until you have reached your ultimate destination. A baby gate across the bedroom door can help the process by limiting access while still allowing your dog to see, hear and smell which can make the separation easier for him.

This can be a tough nut to crack so it's really important that you start as early as possible to give yourselves the greatest chance of success and a dog who can sleep happily at night away from you by the time baby arrives.

Car Transport Location

This is another change that is easily overlooked. Where does your dog travel in the car? If he is used to travelling on the rear seat then that's not going to be appropriate or safe if you will also have a baby car seat there. It might be possible to have baby in front and your dog in the back. That can be an acceptable solution for some families. Or you may decide that a better, longer term solution is for your dog to travel in the boot behind a dog guard or in a crate. As with other changes, this might take a little bit of getting used to so do some trial runs now and see how your dog gets on. It may only take a few car journeys with the added attraction of some treats or a chew to make him feel happy in his new spot. But if it is likely to take a little longer starting now gives you that time.

New Stimuli

New babies bring new stimuli. Stimuli are things your dog can perceive in the environment around them. Babies bring new smells, new sounds, new equipment, more visitors to the home, more strangers in the home. Different dogs will react differently to all of these so it's worth thinking about your dog and whether these new things in his life are likely to excite or worry him. We'll discuss how to introduce new stimuli in more detail in chapter seven but for now just give some thought to how you think your dog may be likely to react and adapt to the new stimuli a baby brings. If you need to refer back to the assessment of your dog's personality which you completed in chapter two.

Summary

Many things in your dog's life will change when your baby joins your family. Change can be challenging for our dogs just as it can be for us. More so, perhaps, since they have no concept of why things have changed, only that they have. Too much change, too quickly is often at the root of the problem behaviours dogs commonly display after the arrival of a baby. Dogs who display problematic behaviours aren't deliberately giving their owners a hard time due to jealousy or stubbornness, their behaviour is a reflection of the fact that they are having a hard time themselves.

You can go a long way to preventing these problems by thinking about how your dog's life might change once you have a baby in the family and then beginning to introduce these changes gently and gradually in advance.

Change is a constant once you have children. Babies develop rapidly and their behaviour and the practicalities of life will change with each developmental stage…. the challenges and changes a newborn brings are different from those you will face with a toddler. Being mindful about how these stages may affect your dog is a great habit to get into and will stand you in good stead for the future.

"Babies grow, dogs age. It's important to adjust for every stage"

Family Paws Parent Education ™

Key Points From This Chapter

- Think about the many ways in which your dog's lifestyle is likely to be changed by the arrival of a baby. Use the ideas listed in this chapter but remember they're not exhaustive.

  Begin to introduce these changes gently and gradually. The aim is to move towards a 'new normal' so gradually that your dog barely notices the changes.

- Babies develop rapidly and there will be many more changes ahead for you and your dog. Anticipating these changes and adapting as you go is a great mindset to get into right from the outset.

CHAPTER 4

BEHAVIOUR: THE GOOD, THE BAD AND THE UGLY

Dogs do what works for them. It's as simple as that. They don't see behaviours as 'good' or 'bad' simply as ways to either access things they want – food, play, attention – or avoid or escape things they don't like – strange people, other dogs, pain, fear. So in that regard the title of this chapter is tongue in cheek. There aren't 'good' or 'bad' behaviours…there is just behaviour.

There are, however, behaviours which are more or less helpful and appropriate in a home with babies and young children. In this chapter we are going to think about what you would like your dog to do in certain situations, what they can already do and identify any gaps in their training that might need filled.

We'll think about what behaviours are helpful and will make your life easier and less stressful and, in turn, increase your dog's inclusion in family life. We'll also consider how the addition of a baby into the family can have a huge impact on how you view a behaviour. Finally we'll cover how to address more serious behavioural issues like aggressive behaviours towards people, resource guarding etc

What Do You Want Your Dog *To* Do?

In order to plan, and train, effectively we need to have a clear idea of what we want our dogs TO do. It can be tempting to focus on what we DON'T want but you can't teach a dog an "un-behaviour". If we stop or suppress one behaviour it has to be replaced by an alternative behaviour and that alternative might not be something we want! It's far more effective to focus on what we want and then teach that.

Instead of 'not jumping up' we can teach him to keep four feet on the floor, instead of 'not pulling on the lead' we can teach him to walk on a loose lead and instead of 'not barking' we can teach calm behaviours. Focusing on what we want allows us to set clear measurable goals to work towards.

Effective goal setting requires goals to be **SMART** –

Specific	What you want your dog TO do

Measurable	How you are going to define success e.g. my dog sits 9 times out of 10 when I ask him to
Achievable	If your dog has had little training so far then aiming for a 20 minute down stay is unrealistic. Aiming for a settle behind a baby gate might be more realistic
Relevant	Focus on the things that will really help you in your new life as a family. Don't spend time training things that you don't need right now
Time Based	You have limited time so prioritise the things that will have the most benefit to you

Bearing these criteria in mind your next task is to imagine common scenarios with your baby and think about how you would like your dog to behave in those scenarios. Don't think about what you *don't* want; think about what you *do* want.

Here are few examples to get you started –

When… I am pushing the pram

I would like my dog to… walk by my side on a loose lead

Skill needed… loose lead walking

When… my baby is having tummy time on the floor

I would like my dog to… settle in the kitchen

Skill needed… the ability to settle alone

When… I walk into the room holding the baby

I would like my dog to… greet me calmly

Skill needed… the ability to keep four paws on the floor

The next thing I'd like you to do is think about the *less* helpful things your dog currently does and think about what you would rather they did instead.

Instead of… jumping up on me

I would like my dog to… keep his feet on the floor

Instead of… running out of the front door

I would like my dog to… wait at the door

When you have completed both these exercises you may well find that the same skills will both replace existing problematic behaviours and be useful in many different situations. For example, the ability to keep four paws on the floor can be helpful when you enter a room, when friends and family visit your home to see the baby, when you are putting on your dog's lead etc. The thought of teaching your dog new skills may seem overwhelming, especially if you haven't done much previous training together but a few key skills, done well, may be all you need.

What Can Your Dog Already Do?

Now that you have established what you would like your dog to do let's consider the things that your dog can already do which will be helpful and appropriate in a home with a baby. Get your pad and a pen and write down all the helpful behaviours that your dog performs reliably. Write down everything, even if it seems inconsequential. Look back to the answers you gave in chapter two when you assessed your dog's personality and existing behaviour.

Here are some suggestions to get you started –

- My dog responds to his name
- My dog comes when I call him in the house
- My dog comes when I call him outside
- My dog can sit/lie down when I ask
- My dog keeps his paws on the floor when he greets me
- My dog walks beside me on a loose lead
- My dog will get off the furniture if I ask him
- My dog will go to his bed when he is asked
- My dog is calm when he greets people outside
- My dog can settle quietly while we relax and watch tv
- My dog is well housetrained

Now, put this list to one side and over the next few days pay close attention to your dog's behaviour. Observe both how they respond when you ask them to do things but also what behaviour they offer voluntarily and naturally.

Our pre-programmed, hardwired, human negativity bias means we more often overlook all the lovely behaviours our dogs offer us compared to how quickly we notice their unwanted behaviours, even when those problematic behaviours occur far less often. Negativity bias is a phenomenon that means that we pay more attention, and give more weight, to negative experiences than positive ones.

"The mind is like Velcro for negative experiences and Teflon for positive ones"

Dr Rick Hansen

Negativity bias is why we forget a hundred compliments while remembering, verbatim, an insult. It's why we remember failure more than success and it's why we notice negative behaviour in our dogs more than positive behaviour. It's an innate reaction but we can take steps to overcome it by consciously making the effort to notice and acknowledge positive events. Doing so is a skill to be developed like anything else and the more we do it the more we notice the positive things around us.

In our life with our dogs I think there are two huge benefits of training our eye to notice the good stuff more –

- seeing it gives us the opportunity to reward it, thereby making it more likely that the dog will repeat the behaviour more often in the future; and

- being aware and mindful of just how much helpful behaviour our dogs are already offering us re-frames how we view our dogs. Instead of perhaps being labelled as 'disobedient' or 'stubborn' we see them in a more positive light. We can see them as the dogs they really are.

After you have spent a few days observing your dog's behaviour re-visit your list and add any helpful behaviours which you have overlooked or taken for granted. Perhaps your dog responded calmly to sudden noises? Reacted calmly to the doorbell? Left a piece of dropped food when you asked him to? Came back to you while off lead without being called?

Now you have a list of many (probably not all, as there are always things we miss!) of the 'good' behaviours that your dog either does when asked or offers voluntarily.

Next, you are going to compare what your dog can already do against the skills you would like him to have. You'll probably find that your dog already has some of the skills he needs to be able to do the things you'd like him to do, even if you haven't realised it. And you'll also probably find that there are things that he can't currently do reliably or often. Don't panic! That is the point of this exercise.

By now you will have two lists –

- Behaviours you'd like your dog to do which he already does

- Behaviours you'd like your dog to do which he currently doesn't

We are going to use these lists to create a plan which will –

- Teach new behaviours; and

- Strengthen existing behaviours to make them robust and reliable under as many circumstances as possible

We'll look at both of these in more detail in the following chapter.

Perspective is Everything

So far in this chapter we've taken a constructive, positive approach and thought about how we want your dog to behave around your baby. As we've learned focusing on what we want as opposed to what we don't is the most effective way to build a clear, proactive, goal oriented plan.

However, it's worth stopping for a moment and thinking about perspective. How you view some of your dog's behaviour might change when seen through the lens of parenthood. Some things which are acceptable or enjoyable to you now may suddenly seem problematic when a baby or a young child is in the mix. If your dog expresses affection by licking you is that a behaviour that you would want replicated with a child? You may love having your dog sleep on your lap now but how will that work when you are feeding a baby or holding a toddler? It's worth considering whether there are any behaviours which are not currently problematic but which might become so in the future. If there are think what a more appropriate alternative behaviour might be and add that to your training list.

Red Flag Behaviours

There are some behaviour problems, like aggression or resource guarding, which require experienced, professional help. They are far beyond the scope of a book like this and you should not try to address these using advice from books or the internet. Changing aggressive behaviours is a complex task and must be handled by a qualified professional with extensive knowledge and experience of working with aggression in dogs.

Behaviour is a complex, multi-faceted science and the manner in which behaviour modification is carried out can have a huge impact on the long term success of the training. Any solution has to focus on why the dog is behaving as he is, not just on the behaviour itself. The behaviour we can see is the result of your dog's genetics, learning history, environment and other factors like their physical health and wellbeing. Novice owners or inexperienced trainers may focus only on stopping the aberrant behaviour but fail to address the underlying causes behind the behaviour. This is an overly simplistic approach which tackles the symptom but not the cause. Although this approach may work in the short term it will almost certainly result in a resurgence of the original aggressive behaviour at some point in the future.

This is why, if your dog has ever displayed aggressive behaviours towards people like lunging, growling, snapping, biting etc or has aggressively guarded food or other objects, you *must* seek experienced, professional advice and support. The information in this book is not intended in any way to address these serious and potentially dangerous issues.

If you need to find a professional trainer or behaviourist to help you with serious issues like aggressive behaviour (or anything else touched on in this book...remember trainers are there to help you in every aspect of your life with your dog, not just serious behaviour problems) look for a qualified, experienced trainer or behaviourist who uses positive reinforcement training techniques and who is a member of a recognised professional body. This will ensure that they have had their competency and knowledge externally assessed, that they have signed up to a transparent code of ethics, that you are protected by a clear complaints procedure, that they are adequately insured and that the trainer is obliged to undertake continuous professional development.

Organisations to look out for include the Animal and Behaviour Training Council (ABTC), the Association of Pet Behaviour Counsellors (APBC), the Institute of Modern Dog Trainers (IMDT), the Association of Pet Dog Trainers (APDT), the Karen Pryor Academy for Animal Training and Behaviour (KPA) or any behaviourist qualified as a Certified Clinical Animal Behaviourist (CCAB).

Summary

When we are setting goals in any aspect of our lives the most effective way to do that is to focus on what we want, as opposed to what we don't and then make sure those goals are clearly defined and realistic. Training our dogs is no exception to this and taking the time to break things down in a little detail helps make the whole things seem less daunting. "I need to train my dog before the baby comes" sounds a bit overwhelming but "I need to teach my dog to sit when asked and walk on a loose lead" doesn't sound quite so bad! Clear goals also help keep you focused and motivated.

Remember when you are considering what new skills you need to teach your dog that how you view their behaviour may change when you see it through the lens of parenthood. As our perspective changes so does how we view things.

Finally, if your dog has ever displayed aggressive behaviours towards people you must seek professional help. You cannot safely address these behaviours alone or through books or internet advice. Seek a qualified, positive reinforcement professional to help you.

Key Points From This Chapter

- Think about what you want your dog TO do in any given scenario

- Keep your goals SMART – specific, measurable, achievable, relevant and time based

- Compare your goal behaviours against things your dog can already do to create your list of training goals

- Always seek professional advice if you are tackling serious behavioural problems like aggression or resource guarding

CHAPTER 5

BUILDING NEW BEHAVIOUR

"The most reliable way to predict the future is to create it"

Abraham Lincoln

If you are reading this book then you already have a dog (as an aside if you are reading this book because you are pregnant and thinking of getting a dog.... DON'T! Pregnancy is not the time to add a puppy or a new dog to your family) and if you already have a dog the chances are you will have done at least some training with them, perhaps a puppy class or some simple at home training.

In this chapter we are going to learn a little bit about the theory of how dogs learn and consider some different ways in which you can teach them the wanted behaviours you identified in the previous chapter.

An understanding of the principles of how dogs learn is really valuable for every dog owner. Once you understand the principles underpinning behaviour it makes it much easier to teach your dog what you want him to do.

As an aside, the laws of behaviour apply to all species including humans. We can (and should) apply the same kind, ethical approach to teaching using positive reinforcement to our children as well as our dogs.

How Dogs Learn

Dogs (and every other species) learn in two main ways – by association (classical conditioning) and by consequences (operant conditioning). That might sound a bit daunting but these are ways of learning you will already be very familiar with…even if you didn't realise it.

Classical Conditioning

Classical conditioning refers to learning by association; making the link between one thing and another. You might have heard of "Pavlov's Dogs"? Pavlov was a Russian physiologist who noticed that the dogs he used in his experiments began to salivate merely at the sight of the lab assistant who fed them before he actually gave them their food. They had come to associate the person with food which made them salivate even when food wasn't present.

Think about how your dog reacts when he sees you pick up his lead...he's excited, right? The lead elicits a positive emotional reaction. But it's not the lead itself that makes him excited – after all, it's just a 6ft piece of leather. It's what the lead has come to be associated with – a walk, fun, time with you – that's exciting, not the lead itself.

We can use this phenomenon to help our dogs create positive associations with objects, situations, sounds etc. For example, if we feed our dogs tasty treats every time he is in his crate we can help him create a positive association with the crate.

In chapter eight we will talk about how to introduce new stimuli to your dog in a way that helps them feel comfortable. Much of the process outlined in that chapter is based on classical conditioning.

Operant Conditioning

Operant conditioning is learning from experience. Or, to put it another way, learning from the consequences of behaviour. It is the consequences of a behaviour which determine whether or not the behaviour is likely to be performed again. Put simply, if the consequence is favourable the behaviour is likely to happen again (in scientific terms it has been reinforced); if it's unfavourable it's unlikely to be repeated (in scientific terms it has been punished).

So if a dog gets a treat each time he sits he'll be more likely to sit in the future. If you get a shock when you stick your fingers in a socket you're unlikely to try it again!

There are three elements to behaviour, the **ABC**s –

Antecedents – what happens before the behaviour, e.g. asking your dog to "sit"

Behaviour – the behaviour itself e.g. the dog sits

Consequence – what happens after the behaviour e.g. the dog gets a treat

It isn't you asking the dog which makes him sit, it is the combined consequences of all the times before when he has sat when asked. Positive reinforcement training works by adding something rewarding after a wanted behaviour which then makes it more likely that that behaviour will be repeated in the future. It focuses on building what we want by making it rewarding for the learner rather than punishing what we don't want. The maxim to bear in mind is "what gets rewarded gets repeated".

Why Not Punishment?

Imagine you had a friend who kept glancing at their phone when they were talking to you instead of looking at you. If you poked them every time they looked at the phone they might stop looking at it but they wouldn't necessarily look more at you. It would probably also make them move further away from you or avoid you altogether or even retaliate by poking you back.

Although you have successfully punished the behaviour of looking at the phone you haven't taught your friend what behaviour you would prefer, you have probably damaged your relationship and you have run the risk of retaliation in response to the punishment.

We should never use punishment to teach our dogs. It can be effective to change behaviour but it comes with the real risk of significant fallout -

- Punishment runs the risk of damaging your relationship with your dog (would you trust someone who habitually punishes you?)

   Simply suppressing one behaviour may inadvertently create other problem behaviours. For example, we could use punishment to stop our dog jumping at us for attention but he may simply switch to barking at us instead

- Punishment stops behaviour but it doesn't teach the learner what to do

- Punishment creates fear and uncertainty which can make behaviour unpredictable

None of these outcomes are desirable under any conditions but certainly not in a house with a baby. We want our dogs to feel relaxed, safe and secure in their home. A dog who fears punishment and has lost trust in his humans is more likely to live in a state of tension and anxiety which may result in more unpredictable behaviour. And that is the last thing we want.

Having an understanding of the theory behind how dogs learn allows us to see more clearly how we can encourage and strengthen the behaviours we want our dogs to have. Positive reinforcement (making wanted behaviours rewarding) is not only a kind way to teach but it's also hugely effective and will result in a stronger relationship with your dog.

Building New Behaviours

Now that we understand a little more about how to build and change behaviour using positive reinforcement we're going to consider some of the different routes you can take to teach your dog. In the previous chapter you identified the gaps which exist in your dog's learning so let's consider ways in which you might go about filling them.

I am not going to go into huge detail about how to train lots of different behaviours (although I have included a short appendix with simple training notes on some basic, but versatile, skills that will be universally useful to all dog owners). There are many great training books and online resources available which go into greater detail of how to train specific behaviours than I can here; you'll find a list of suggested resources later in this book.

Train SMART, Not Hard

Life is busy. Work, partners, friends, household chores.... Sometimes our busy modern lives get in the way of things we know we should be doing – like going to the gym or training our dogs – and we end up feeling guilty because another day has gone by and we haven't got round to it. Going to the gym I can't help you with, but finding a flexible, easy way to build teaching your dog into your day, I can!

There's a really simple, powerful way to teach our dogs what behaviours we want without having to find the time for formal training sessions. It's called SMART50 training and it's outlined in "Plenty In Life Is Free", a wonderful book by amazingly talented animal trainer, Kathy Sdao. It is one of my absolute favourite ways to easily build training into our busy lives.

SMART training, or **S**ee **M**ark **A**nd **R**eward **T**raining, can be summarised as follows –

"Fifty times each day reward your dog for doing something you want to see more of"

Each morning set out a bowl with around 50 small treats in it. You can use some of your dog's daily food allowance for this instead of feeding it to them in a bowl. Then –

- **SEE the wanted behaviour** – train your eye to notice when your dog is doing something you'd like to see more of....for example being settled quietly, or having 4 feet on the floor, or standing calmly in front of you, or giving you eye contact, or walking calmly on the lead, or coming when called, sitting when asked etc. It doesn't matter whether you asked for the behaviour or not. If you like it you are going to reward it.

- **MARK the wanted behaviour** – 'mark' means to use a clicker or consistent marker word (something short, clear & concise like 'good', 'yes', 'nice') the instant the dog offers the behaviour you like. By doing this we're pointing out the good behaviour to the dog and helping him learn exactly what behaviour is earning him a treat

- **REWARD the wanted behaviour** – what gets rewarded gets repeated so paying your dog well for offering wanted behaviours will increase the strength & frequency of those behaviours in the future. And the more wanted behaviour we get the less unwanted behaviour we get. Win – win.

Your goal is to empty the bowl by the end of the day. You can choose to reinforce only one goal behaviour or simply reward any wanted behaviour (this is my preference). If you do this daily within a week you'll have reinforced 350 instances of good behaviour. Within a month 1,500 instances. Maintain the habit for a year and you'll have reinforced over 18,000 wanted behaviours. It's a simple, easy, effective way to train on the hoof without setting aside specific time and it has a real positive impact on behaviour.

SMART50 trains the human end of the lead as much as the canine end – it teaches us to notice and reward the good instead of that all too human trait of focusing on the negative (there's that negativity bias cropping up again....). Seeking out the positive has a profound effect on our own attitudes and wellbeing and it's a habit that can spill over into other aspects of our lives with beneficial effects.

I am a huge fan of this approach to training and at a busy time in your life it is achievable. Overly complex or time consuming training plans get left undone but this approach can be incorporated into even the busiest schedule easily.

Books & Courses

There are many great training books and online courses available which not only explain how to train specific behaviours but also teach owners the principles of learning. Once you understand these principles you can apply them throughout the rest of your dog's life to the huge benefit of both of you.

These can be the least expensive of the learning

options open to you.

Classes

A good training class can be a great way to kick start your dog's learning especially if the gaps you need to fill are fairly generic, foundation behaviours like sit, lead walking etc.

Signs of a good class would include –

- It is run by an experienced, qualified trainer using positive reinforcement techniques
- Small class sizes to ensure sufficient personal attention
- A relaxed atmosphere with no pressure on the dogs to 'perform'

The downside to classes is that you will generally be following a set curriculum which means you may spend time learning things which aren't your priority. Depending on how much time you have before your baby is due that may not be ideal.

One to One Training

One to one training with a professional trainer has one significant advantage over other methods as it allows you to tailor your training sessions to precisely what you want to work on. In a time limited situation that can be very useful as it allows you to direct your resources exactly where you need them. There can be a perception that professional dog trainers are only there to help owners with serious, complex issues like aggression but that couldn't be further from the truth. Trainers help clients with a huge range of problems (and many with none at all). A few sessions with a trainer can set you well on the road to building reliable behaviours and help you avoid novice mistakes.

If you are choosing a trainer to help you, ensure they are an experienced, qualified trainer who uses positive reinforcement techniques and that they are a member of a reputable professional organisation. The downside of personal training is that it is the most expensive option available due to the bespoke, personal service you receive.

Summary

Having an understanding of how dogs learn enables you to teach your dog new things and strengthen existing behaviours more effectively. We can harness the power of both classical and operant conditioning to encourage the behaviours we want to see from our dogs. Similarly, having an understanding of the potential fallout from the use of punishment can encourage us to focus more on using positive reinforcement to teach what we want rather than punishment to stop what we don't.

There are many learning options open to you to help you teach your dog new behaviours – everything from books and online courses to bespoke personal training. Each has their advantages and disadvantages and the right option for you will depend on how many new skills you need to teach your dog, the complexity of the skills you need to teach your dog, the time you have available and your budget. One of the simplest, easiest and most effective ways to begin building new behaviour is to train yourself to notice wanted behaviour and reward it.

Key Points From This Chapter

- Dogs learn by association (classical conditioning) and by consequences (operant conditioning)

- Positive reinforcement builds and strengthens behaviour by making the consequences of that behaviour rewarding

- Classical and operant conditioning applies to all species – human and non-human

- Punishment has potential fallout

- There are many learning options to help you teach your dog new behaviours

- Training your eye to notice the good can be a wonderful foundation to build upon

CHAPTER 6

(BABY) PROOFING BEHAVIOUR

Cast your mind back to when you were learning to drive. After a few lessons you might feel able to drive fairly competently in a quiet area with little other traffic and few junctions. 'Yay...I can drive!', you think. But if your instructor took you to the city centre, in rush hour, in the driving rain the chances are that the combination of distractions and the level of difficulty would be too great and your newly found skills would fall apart. It's not that you can't drive.... you just can't drive under those circumstances.

You'll probably have experienced the same thing with your dog when you were teaching them new skills as a puppy. They might have been able to sit in your home but not respond to the same cue outside. Or come back to you beautifully when you call them in a quiet park but not respond when there are other dogs in the vicinity. The different environment meant the behaviour weakened.

There are two stages to becoming fluent in a new skill – acquiring the skill and then perfecting the skill. In dog training lingo 'proofing' means taking the skill from the acquisition stage and perfecting it until it can be performed reliably in any environment under (almost) any conditions.

Let's assume you are teaching your dog to sit. When we are teaching our dogs we often, inadvertently, go into 'training mode'. We practice in the same room of the house, perhaps at the same time each day, with treats in a certain place, standing facing our dog...in short, we create a fixed picture for our dog of what 'sit' looks like. Although, to us, the most pertinent part of that picture is our verbal cue of 'sit' for the dog it is ALL equally relevant. Changing one piece of the jigsaw changes the whole picture for them which is why a dog may sit beautifully when you are standing in front of him in the kitchen but be unable to perform the same behaviour if you are sitting down in the park. If we make our training picture too rigid we make it harder for our dogs to be able to generalise a behaviour from one environment to another.

In the previous chapter you identified helpful behaviours that your dog can already perform. Now we are going to learn how to polish and strengthen those existing behaviours to make them as robust and reliable as possible by 'proofing' them.

There are six elements to proofing –

- Precision – what a behaviour looks like

- Latency – the time between you asking for a behaviour and your dog doing it

- Speed – the speed with which the dog does the behaviour

- Distractions – things in the environment that compete with your cues

- Duration – how long the behaviour lasts for

- Distance – the distance from the handler at which the behaviour can be performed

For the purposes of this book we are most interested in what are collectively known as the 3Ds - distractions, duration and distance. Let's look at each in turn.

Distractions

It's one thing asking your dog to perform a behaviour in the calm and predictable environment of your own home or in a situation where he's performed it a hundred times before. It's quite another to ask them to do it under new conditions or with distractions nearby. As we've learned dogs don't always generalise behaviours well to new environments or when we change the 'picture' they are used to.

A distraction can be anything a dog can perceive – a sight, a sound, a smell, a touch. And, as we've learned, it can also be a change in the usual 'picture' that your dog sees.

Let's imagine that one of the helpful behaviours you've identified your dog can already do is to lie down when asked. We want to make that behaviour bulletproof so that when you give the cue 'lie down' your dog does it every single time regardless of what else is going on around him.

A cue is the word you say (or the hand signal you use) to signal to your dog what behaviour you would like them to do. The first step in building a strong, reliable behaviour is teaching your dog to respond to that cue no matter what else is going on in the environment. To do that we need your dog to understand that the most relevant thing to him is the cue itself – in this case, 'lie down' - and nothing else. We can do this by varying things as much as possible while the cue remains constant.

You are going to start practising the behaviours your dog can already do in short training sessions. Keep the sessions short – five minutes at a time is plenty - but frequent. Five minutes three times a day is more effective than one session lasting fifteen minutes and also more achievable for you. Short sessions can be squeezed in while you wait for the kettle to boil or in an advert break. Use high value treats and reward your dog every time he gets it right.

- Start by varying things like your body position and body movement. Ask your dog to 'lie down' when you are standing up, sitting on the floor, sitting in a chair, have your back to your dog, while you are standing still, waving your arms in the air, standing on one leg, walking about the room or even lying flat on your back on the floor! Be as creative as you like! Be sure to reward your dog every time he performs the behaviour. If he gets stuck or begins to make mistakes take a break and then start with something a bit easier the next time. By doing this exercise you are helping your dog to understand that it is the cue 'lie down' which is the most relevant thing for him and not what you happen to be doing when you say it.

- Once your dog is responding reliably begin to add in more distractions or changes. Ask for the behaviour in different locations – different rooms of the house, outside in the garden, at the park etc. Cue him to perform the behaviour when the television is on, or your partner is moving around, or the doorbell rings.

- Practice giving your cue while you are holding a baby doll or a blanket rolled up to resemble a swaddled baby. You're not trying to fool your dog into thinking you have a baby (they're not daft!) but the chances are they've never seen you holding an object that way and that one small difference can change the picture enough to confuse them.

- Introduce distractions gradually in order to keep your dog successful. Asking him to 'lie down' in a busy park is unlikely to be successful if he can't do it under lesser distractions. It's important to keep our dogs successful when we are teaching them – if they start to make mistakes, they receive fewer rewards and in turn they become de-motivated and disengaged. We all like getting things right, including our dogs!

Repeat this process with all the behaviours your dog already knows in order to really strengthen the reliability of their response.

Duration

Duration is the amount of time that a behaviour goes on for. It can relate to the length of time a static behaviour is held, for example staying on a bed, or to the length of time a moving behaviour goes on for, for example the length of time your dog can walk on a loose lead.

Increasing the amount of time your dog can do some behaviours for can be really useful and can enable you to include the dog in family life more easily. For example, a dog who can go to his bed and stay there while you change a nappy allows you to focus on your baby and means the dog is less likely to be removed from the room.

We teach a dog to perform a behaviour for longer in small, achievable increments that keep your dog engaged and successful.

The key points to successfully increase the duration of a behaviour are –

- Small increases. Don't get greedy and push for too much too quickly. If your dog can already stay in his bed for two minutes don't try to jump to five minutes. Try two and a half minutes. The easier we make it for him, the more he'll get it right, which means he'll get more rewards, which means he'll be more likely to settle for longer in the future.

- When you reach your target time for each repetition reward your dog with a high value reward like sausage or cheese. You need to make it worth your dog's time!

- For moving behaviours, like walking on a lead, you can measure either in time or in the number of steps, distance etc. Again, the key is increasing your criteria in achievable increments.

- If you are working to increase duration, reduce distractions. If you are trying to teach your dog to stay in bed longer start when the house is quiet, not when it's busy. You want to set your dog up to succeed.

- Don't consistently increase duration at every repetition. If we do that we just make each repetition harder which can get discouraging for your dog and runs the risk they'll disengage. Although we want to maintain an overall upward trajectory you can 'ping pong' around by mixing up some longer and some shorter durations. This gives your learner some 'easy wins' and keeps them motivated and engaged. An overall upward trajectory is achieved but it also incorporates some easy repetitions which will keep your learner in the game.

Again, keep sessions short but frequent. Your dog will enjoy them more and you'll be more likely to do them.

Distance

The final element of building fluency in a behaviour is distance. There will be times when your dog is not close beside you but you want to ask him to do something. For example if you are sitting feeding the baby and your dog starts barking at the window you might want to ask him to go to his bed from where you are, without having to get up and move towards him.

The simplest way to teach your dog this is to start in close proximity to each other and gradually increase the distance -

- Start standing or sitting beside your dog. Cue the behaviour and reward him if he performs it successfully. Next move ever so slightly away, ask for the behaviour again and reward for success.

- For some dogs this might mean merely shifting your weight backwards slightly or rocking back on one foot. That's fine...we need to start where he can be successful and go from there. Repeat, gradually increasing the distance you move and always at a pace that keeps your dog successful

- If your dog is already able to perform a 'stay' behaviour you can also use that as a 'jumping off point' to add distance. Ask your dog to 'stay', move away a short distance then ask for the behaviour you are working on. Gradually increase the distance you move away before cueing the second behaviour.

Summary

By taking a little time to practice known behaviours under different conditions and by gradually making those conditions more challenging we can transform them from being ok to being awesome. Having behaviours that are strong and reliable under many different conditions means that you have predictability and confidence about how your dog is likely to behave which, in turn, will help you feel calm and in control.

Key Points From This Chapter

- Being too rigid in the training 'picture' we present to our dogs can make it difficult for them to transfer behaviours from one environment to another

- There are two stages to becoming fluent at any skill – acquiring the skill and perfecting the skill

- By gradually adding and increasing distractions, duration and distance and rewarding your dog well for successful behaviour you can transform existing behaviours from ok to awesome

CHAPTER 7

DO YOU SPEAK DOG?

"Dogs do speak, but only to those who know how to listen"

Anonymous

One of the main concerns of a dog owning family about to have a baby is "will our baby be safe around our dog". It's a natural concern and a valid one. Dogs, of any temperament and breed, have the potential to do harm.

Children are twice as likely to be bitten than the general population and the vast majority of those bites, around 80%, occur in the home from a known dog. Statistically, if your child is bitten it will almost certainly be a bite from a family pet. Dog bites in children are also more likely to have serious long term consequences as they occur more often to the face or neck compared to adults who are more likely to be bitten on the extremities. Most dog bites to children are the result of a combination of a failure in supervision and a lack of understanding of canine body language.

I don't include these facts in order to scare or alarm you but it's important to understand that the two most effective ways to keep your child safe around your dog are –

- adequate and appropriate supervision; and

- an understanding of your dog's body language

We'll discuss supervision in further detail in chapter ten but in this chapter we are going to learn more about how your dog uses his body to communicate how he is feeling.

Dogs are social creatures and generally want to avoid conflict wherever possible. Most dogs don't want to employ aggressive behaviours if they can avoid it since aggression always runs the risk that the dog himself will be hurt. Their first response to conflict is rarely a growl or a snap. They will almost always try to de-escalate tense situations by displaying smaller, more subtle signals first. However, we often don't recognise these low level signals for what they are and so we ignore them or misinterpret them. As a result our dog feels he has no option but to escalate to more overt, obvious aggressive responses like growling, snapping and eventually biting in order to resolve the conflict.

Having an understanding of the more subtle signs a dog gives when he is feeling threatened or uncomfortable gives us the opportunity to intervene at an earlier stage and avoid any escalation to growling and biting.

One other important reason for parents to have an understanding of body language is to be able to teach your children. We can't teach what we don't understand ourselves and being able to see when a dog is uncomfortable is a vital skill for children living with a dog.

Learning How To Read Your Dog

The first step in learning to read your dog more effectively is having a clear picture of what 'normal' looks like. Observe him when there is nothing much going on and he is relaxed. Look at his natural tail carriage, how he holds his ears and what his mouth looks like. Dogs display their emotional state with their bodies so having this picture clear in your head makes it easier to notice when that emotional state begins to change.

Dogs use their eyes, ears, tails, muzzle and sometimes their whole body to communicate their feelings and intentions so let's look at each of these in turn.

Body Part	Body Language	Possible Interpretation
Eyes	Soft eyes; no sign of tension	Relaxed, comfortable
	Hard stare with sustained eye contact	Confrontational, threatening
	Averting their gaze by turning their head away from something (often something approaching)	Uncomfortable, wants the approach to stop, needs a break
	"Whale Eye" – whites of the eyes showing, head turned away from the direction the dog is looking; often accompanied by a very still, 'frozen' body	Stressed, threatened, feeling trapped
	Pinned back close	Anxious, worried,

Ears	to the head	fearful
	Pricked forward	Focused, alert
Mouths	Open, soft, tongue relaxed	Relaxed, comfortable
	Mouth open, lip corners pulled back horizontally in to a tight 'grin, tongue wide and scooped, often accompanied by panting	Anxious, stressed
	Closed, tight mouth with tension in the face	Tense
	Lips pulled up vertically revealing teeth, tense face, wrinkled muzzle, growling or snarling	Very stressed, ready to escalate to physical aggression
	Lip lick, flicking tongue around lips and up and over nose	Worried, uncomfortable, trying to de-escalate a situation
	Yawning	Uncomfortable,

		worried, trying to de-escalate a situation, trying to reduce tension
Tail	Neutral	Relaxed
	Tucked under between back legs	Anxious, worried, fearful
	Erect, upright	Alert and/or tense
	Helicopter wag – high, circular, accompanied by loose, wriggly body	Happy
	Wide, loose wags	Generally relaxed
	Tight, stiff wags	Generally tense, stressed
Body	Loose, soft muscles	Relaxed, comfortable
	Tense, stiff, frozen	Tense, threatening, ready to escalate to physical aggression
	Lying on side with belly exposed, tail	Submissive, feeling threatened

tucked or still	
Shaking off (whole body shake starting at his head and progressing down the spine and tail)	Release of stress after a tense (or exciting) experience, self-soothing or calming

Context is Everything!

When interpreting body language it's really important to take into account three key elements –

- always look at what the dog's entire body is doing and not just one sign in isolation. What is the dog's overall body language, behaviour and demeanour telling you? You need to put all the pieces of the puzzle together to see the whole picture clearly

- Context is everything! Look at what else is going on in the environment as well as specific body movements. If your dog has just finished his dinner when he licks his lips he's probably just licking his lips!

- Remember that body posture, tail carriage and ear carriage will vary based on breed and a dog's individuality. A greyhound or whippet may have a naturally tucked tail while a pug's tail is naturally curled over his back. My own dog, Charlie, has a very upright tail at all times so, for him, that doesn't necessarily indicate alertness.

Look For The Subtle Signs

The signals which are most often missed are the initial subtle signs that a dog is becoming uncomfortable – the head turns, lip licks and yawns. Social media is flooded with 'cute' videos of dogs and babies where, if you know what to look for, you can see that the dogs are not feeling comfortable and trying to communicate that. If we are unaware of these signals we run the risk that the dog may feel they have no option but to escalate to more overt aggressive behaviours like growling or snapping.

Watch your dog to observe if and when he displays these behaviours. Noting when they occur gives you valuable information about the situations your dog finds enjoyable or stressful and the more you understand that the more you will understand your dog. And it's understanding what your dog finds challenging or worrying that allows you to manage situations, intervene at an early stage if needed and keep everyone safe.

Summary

When dogs growl, snap at or bite children it's common to hear people say "it came out of the blue" but there are almost always signals which preceded the snap or the bite which were missed. Dogs rarely opt for a bite as their first response to a situation. They will usually try to de-escalate a conflict peacefully first. Only when those tactics fail will they employ more aggressive tactics.

A good understanding of your dog's body language together with appropriate supervision are the two key factors in creating a safe and conflict free environment.

When interpreting a dog's body language bear in mind what is normal given their breed and individual characteristics. Take into account the context in which the behaviour is happening and look at the dog's entire body and manner rather than focusing on just one body part or signal. Looking at the big picture will help you more accurately interpret what your dog is communicating.

Key Points From This Chapter

- An understanding of body language is essential to create a safe environment for children around dogs

- Look at the dog's entire body; not just one body part when assessing how they are feeling or what they are communicating

- Bear in mind what 'normal' looks like given an individual dog's breed and physical characteristics

- Consider the context the behaviour is happening in; don't look at it in isolation

CHAPTER 8

INTRODUCING NEW THINGS

When your dog was a pup you probably heard a lot about the importance of socialising them well in order for them to feel confident about all the new things they were experiencing in the world around them – different types of people, other dogs, traffic, other animals etc.

Most people tend to be very aware of the importance of introducing new objects and new experiences to a puppy gradually and gently but we don't always take the same care and consideration when introducing new things to an older dog. In this chapter we're going to look at how to do just that.

Behaviour doesn't happen in a vacuum…it happens in response to the stimuli around us. Stimuli are anything that we can perceive – sights, sounds, smells, sensations etc. If we are cold we put on an extra layer, if the television is too loud we turn it down, if the doorbell rings our dog barks. All of these behaviours are a response to stimuli in our environment.

When your dog was a puppy they may have been initially hesitant or, alternatively, very excited about things which they now pay little attention to – traffic noise, the vacuum cleaner, new people etc. Repeated exposure to all the new things around him at a pace your pup could cope with meant that he became habituated to them and, eventually, they no longer elicited a fearful or excited response. They became neutral.

Babies bring with them a lot of new stimuli that dogs may not have experienced before – new sounds, new movements, new objects. These new stimuli may be interesting or exciting or worrying for your dog and, depending on their reaction, may trigger behaviours which won't be helpful when you have a baby in the home. If your dog barks every time the baby cries or startles when the wheels of the pram move that's a problem you really don't need! How can we avoid these potential problems? The answer, just as with a puppy, is repeated, gentle exposure to the new stimuli paired with rewarding the behaviours we want to encourage.

The areas where I most commonly see new parents experiencing difficulty with their dog's behaviour in response to new stimuli are the baby itself, new equipment and objects and new sounds. Let's look in more detail at each of these in turn.

Babies and Children

Many dogs have had little previous direct experience of babies or young children so it's unsurprising that they may be very interested, or possibly worried, by a new little bundle which moves oddly, makes loud, unpredictable noises and is often being carried around by the dog's owner. In almost every way a newborn is radically different to any human your dog has met before so it can be hard to gauge in advance what their response to a baby is likely to be. Introducing babies and young children in a gradual controlled way will give you information about how your dog is likely to react to your baby and allow you to plan accordingly.

A simple way to begin this process is to start to exercise your dog in areas where you know young children will be. Walk your dog past a playpark or a school playground. Pay close attention to whether he acknowledges the children's movement or activity at any stage and at what distance. Think back to the previous chapter and observe his body language. Is his body language relaxed and inquisitive or alert and tense? If he is showing an interest in the children can you identify what he is reacting to? Is it fast movement? Is it high pitched laughing or shouting? It's really important when you are doing this to ensure that you are working within your dog's comfort zone. If your dog is either showing signs of being anxious about the children or becoming totally over excited and frantic in their presence then increase your distance until your dog is calmer. Then reward any calm behaviour your dog displays in the presence of children – calm observation, disengagement from the children, focus on you etc. As your dog displays more relaxed, disinterested behaviours gradually decrease the distance from the children, making sure to always remain within your dog's comfort zone. If you begin to see any signs of anxiety or overexcitement you've probably moved too close too quickly or stayed there just a little too long so give your dog a break then go back a step by moving a little farther away next time.

When your dog is calm and relaxed around children at a distance you can begin to introduce closer interactions. If you have friends or family with older children ask if you can meet up with them to give your dog the opportunity to meet children in closer proximity. Ask the children to ignore your dog initially and simply let him observe while you reward any calm, settled behaviours he offers. If he remains calm and relaxed allow closer interactions, making sure first that the children understand how to pet a dog – use one hand, pet from collar to tail for just a few seconds, then pause to allow the dog the choice to initiate more petting or move away. As before assess his body language to ensure he's relaxed and comfortable and stop interactions if he shows any signs of anxiety or over excitement. I find it helpful to introduce dogs to older children first as they are more predictable in their movements and better able to understand and comply with any instructions you give them. Once you are confident that your dog is happy around older children you can then go on and introduce younger children in the same way.

Some dogs will sail through this process and display calm, appropriate behaviours around children right from the start. But what do you do if your dog does display signs of anxiety or over excitement in the presence of children? The general process of desensitisation outlined above remains the same –

- Start at a distance your dog is comfortable with

- Reward all calm behaviours in the presence of the children

- Gradually move closer in small increments which your dog can cope with

However, because your dog is starting from a more extreme response, changing how he feels will take longer and will probably require much smaller incremental changes. In this case I would highly recommend that you work with a professional, positive reinforcement trainer or behaviour consultant who will be able to guide you through the process and offer you expert advice.

Objects and Equipment

Prams, bouncers, baby gyms, slings, cribs, baby gates – for such tiny creatures babies bring a lot of kit with them! Not only will many of these objects be things your dog has never seen before but lots of baby equipment also has moving parts or is colourful or noisy which may be very exciting or a bit worrying for your dog depending on their personality. It's always worth remembering that lots of this equipment is specifically designed to stimulate the senses so what's interesting for your baby may also be interesting for your dog!

Whether your dog is excited by the new equipment or worried by it the end goal is the same – disinterested neutrality. We want the new equipment to be 'just there'. Just a part of the furniture in the same way as anything else in your home. How we do that is much the same as the process already outlined for reactions to children. If your dog is excited by the equipment then we want to reward calm interaction with it or disengaging from it. And if your dog is worried by it we want to reward calm investigation of it and then calm behaviours around it.

Bringing the equipment into your home before your baby is born will help you gauge your dog's reaction and allow them time to explore the object safely while there's no baby involved! If possible, place the new object somewhere there is enough space around the object to allow your dog freedom to move away and avoid them feeling cornered or hemmed in. Don't lure or cajole them to investigate the object...just let them approach, or not, in their own time. If the object moves or makes noises – like a pram or a baby gym, for example – let your dog experience that. Start to initiate noise or movement when the dog is at a distance to the object rather than when they are right next to it. You can increase proximity and range of movement if your dog is relaxed and calm but you want to avoid startling them unavoidably. If an item is portable then place it in different areas of the house to habituate your dog to its presence in different areas.

Sounds

Babies are noisy! If you've ever tried to settle a baby who just won't stop crying or been on a plane with a crying baby you'll know just how hard to ignore it can be. Crying is an evolutionary behaviour designed to ensure the survival of the baby by eliciting attention and care from a parent. So it makes sense that it should be a sound that is hard to ignore. Both human and non-human animals cry and the acoustic pattern of crying is similar regardless of species. Babies of all species also cry in similar contexts – discomfort, hunger or separation from a caregiver. Given these similarities it's not surprising that some dogs may be unsettled by, or inquisitive about, a baby's cry. Introducing them to the sound in a controlled way can help overcome any anxiety your dog may have about a crying baby. If you know that your dog is sensitive to some sounds then this training is a 'must do' but it's also worth doing for dogs who don't generally display any strong reaction to sounds for the reasons outlined above. A baby's cry has evolved to trigger a response and so even a dog who is not fazed at all by other sounds may be triggered by a baby's cry.

There are many sources of good recordings of baby noise – YouTube has many or there are specific sound training apps which offer a range of noises, including crying. Play these to your dog, starting at a low volume, and pair the sound with treats, calm petting or gentle play. Play the track periodically throughout the day and keep sessions short. If your dog displays no adverse reaction than you can begin to gradually increase the volume. Remember, as before, the key thing is to move at your dog's pace and never push them if they are displaying any signs of anxiety. Once your pup is used to the noise you can mix things up a bit. Wrap up a baby doll or a teddy in blanket, pop your phone inside while you play crying noises, and shush it while you rock or pace as you might if you were comforting a crying baby. Practice some simple cues like 'sit' or 'go to bed' while you hold your crying 'baby'. You might feel a bit daft but this gives your dog controlled exposure to the new things to come and allows you to see how he is likely to react.

Summary

Many of the new stimuli which accompany a baby involve movement or noise. These may be naturally interesting for some dogs or worrying for others. Remember, forewarned is forearmed, so it's helpful to know in advance how your dog is likely to react in order that you can address any potential problems well ahead of time.

The key with introducing your dog to any new thing – children, objects, sounds, anything – is to do it gradually and slowly and always move at your dog's pace. You may complete these activities and find your dog takes everything in his stride. In which case, great! You can relax in the knowledge you've prepared your dog as best you can. Time spent in preparation is never wasted.

If you discover that your dog is excited or worried by something new don't panic. It's far better to discover this in advance than being surprised by an unexpected reaction when your baby is here. Don't rush, take things slowly and reach out to a professional trainer if you need guidance and support.

Key Points From this Chapter

- Introduce new things gradually

- Never lure or cajole your dog in order to encourage interaction with something that worries them

- Always work at your dog's pace

CHAPTER 9

PRACTICAL PLANNING

"The secret to getting ahead is getting started"

Mark Twain

I'm a planner! I am always writing lists of jobs to be done, calls to be made, emails to be sent. It gives me a feeling of satisfaction and control to tick things off my lists as I accomplish them. Knowing that everything which needs to be done has been done allows me to relax and focus on other things.

One of the primary aims of this book is to make the early days of parenthood in a home with a dog and a baby as stress free as it can possibly be. Those first few days and weeks can be chaotic and time seems to trickle through your fingers without much to show for it. Caring for a newborn while attending to your own needs and those of your dog is pretty all consuming and leaves little time for other things. So taking some time to get ahead, get organised and tick some things off your to do list means you can focus on more important things in the knowledge that day to day practicalities have been taken care of.

In this chapter we'll look at some practical things you can do ahead of time to make things easier later on.

Appointments

Check ahead on your calendar and if your dog is due to visit the vet or the groomer around the time your baby is due, or in the weeks afterwards, make those appointments now. If you can, bring them forward so that they are out of the way before your baby is here. If your dog is on medication or supplements make sure you have a large enough supply to see you through the first few weeks at least. You'll be glad of fewer errands to run when the time comes.

If you are planning to engage a trainer to work with you and your dog to help you prepare for your baby's arrival start the process as far in advance as you can. The earlier you start working with them the greater the results you will see by the time baby is here. Bear in mind also that good trainers often have a waiting list so contact your chosen trainer as far in advance as possible to ensure that they have availability for you.

Household Chores

Any home with a baby is likely to need baby gates fitted in key places at some stage. Although you won't need to limit the baby's movement initially it can be helpful to install baby gates now as they are a great way to help you safely manage your dog around your baby as we'll see in a future chapter. Now is a great time to find gates that suit your home and have them installed. Doing this in advance has a number of advantages beyond simply ticking a DIY job off your list. It allows your dog time to get used to the presence of the gates well in advance of the baby's arrival. If you are going to create dog free zones then putting those boundaries in place using gates now means that your dog has time to become used to being excluded from these areas. Having the gates in place ahead of time also gives you the opportunity to get into the habit of using them to limit your dog's movement around the house so that it becomes second nature by the time the baby is here.

Stock Pile!

Stock up on your dog's food now. If you have adequate storage space order a few months' supply. Many companies now offer scheduled regular deliveries of dog food so investigate whether this is an option for your brand. Knowing that your dog's food is being automatically delivered each month means that's one less thing for you to have to organise.

Bulk buy things like poo bags, treats and chews. Many large online retailers sell multipacks of products like these which will keep you in stock for weeks or even months ahead.

If you need to purchase any new equipment for your dog – a new lead to replace the pram-incompatible extending lead, for example, do it now.

In a later chapter we will discuss the importance of adequate enrichment for your dog. We can add a lot of interest and activity to their life by feeding them using interactive toys like KONGs ™ or Snufflemats ™. Having a varied selection of these will keep your dog engaged and give them something constructive to do which will, in turn, make your life so much easier. A good pet shop or online retailer will have a huge selection of enrichment toys and puzzle feeders so consider investing in a selection of toys. Quality dog toys and feeders can be expensive but they are worth their weight in gold when they keep your dog occupied and engaged. A bored dog and a new baby are not a good mix!

Many of us batch cook and freeze meals to make life

more convenient for us so why not do something similar for your dog? Make up a selection of stuffed KONGs ™ and pop them in the freezer now so that they are ready and waiting when you need them. Making them up as you go is something you're likely to struggle for the time to do so make use of your freezer and prepare ahead of time.

Walker / Day Care

Employing a dog walker or sending your dog to day care can be a great way to ensure your dog is getting regular exercise and a degree of structure in his life while also allowing you some dog-free time with your baby. Even if you don't currently use a dog walker or a day care service it is something worth considering as they can be hugely helpful to lighten the load in those initial busy months and take some pressure off you.

If this is something you plan to do then start searching for a good walker or day care now. Finding just the right person or place can take time as the quality of providers varies greatly. Ask around for a personal recommendation. If you are working with a trainer ask their advice about which option might best suit your dog.

Good walkers or day cares often have waiting lists

so start looking well ahead of time to maximise your chances of securing a place for your dog with the right person. Ideally have your dog begin going out on walks or attending day care well ahead of time so that if they take time to settle or if you need to rethink your plans you have time in hand.

Labour Plans

Whether you are planning a hospital birth or a home birth you'll need to consider where your dog will be and who will be caring for him while you are in labour.

Is your dog going to remain at home or will you ask friends or family to look after him? Or perhaps have him cared for in kennels or by a pet sitter?

One of the complications when making these decisions is that, although we can plan our births as much as we like, it is an unpredictable process. We can't predict exactly when we will go into labour, how long labour will last or how long we may have to remain in hospital afterwards. My first daughter was born prematurely and we had to remain in hospital for over a week afterwards. Neither of those things were in the plan and so our plans for caring for our dog had to adapt. And quickly!

Some things to consider when you are deciding on your plans for your dog –

- Are you planning a home birth or a hospital birth?

- If it's a home birth do you want your dog at home with you? Is it suitable for your dog to remain at home? Will he cope with strangers in the house? Will the sound of mum in pain or potentially distressed be upsetting for him? Will separation from the activity in the home be a problem for him? Will having your dog in the home be a distraction for you?

- If you are having a hospital birth will you keep your dog at home with you until you leave for hospital? Can they be left happily alone when you need to leave?

- If you have a dog who struggles to be left alone then do you have someone close at hand who will be available at short notice to care for your dog?

- If your labour is long and your partner stays with you in hospital do you have someone on call to either go to your home to care for your dog or pick your dog up and take him to their home?

- If you have to remain in hospital for some time after the birth do you plan for your partner to spend the day in hospital with you? If so you will need someone else to care for your dog while your partner is with you. Or will your partner only visit at set times in which case perhaps your dog could remain at home with your partner?

- Would kennels or boarding suit your dog or would they be more comfortable in their own home with a pet sitter?

- If you are booking a home boarder, pet sitter or kennel can they be flexible about dates? Only 4% of babies arrive on their due date so flexibility is a must!

There are no right or wrong answers to these questions. The right option for you will depend on lots of factors including the proximity of reliable friends and family, proximity to the hospital, whether you have trusted professionals like a dog walker who already help you care for your dog. The important thing is to have a plan. And a plan B because babies are unpredictable. If you've arranged for your friend to care for your dog and your baby decides to arrive three weeks ahead of schedule (or three weeks late) while your friend is away on business you need a backup plan!

No matter what your plan turns out to be I'd recommend packing a bag for your dog about a month in advance of your due date. Do it at the same time you pack your own hospital bag! Include enough food for the time your dog is likely to be away, a couple of bowls, a few toys, some treats and a couple of long lasting chews. Also include an information sheet with details of your dog's routine, any particular likes / dislikes / fears etc, details of any medication if relevant, your vet's contact details and your own contact details, if the person doesn't already have them. Even if you plan for your dog to be staying at home things can be unpredictable and you don't want to be running round trying to pack a bag for your dog when you are in labour. Finally, if someone is coming to your home to care for your dog or pick up your dog make sure they have keys to your house well in advance.

Summary

A little time making some simple, practical preparations means you can tick those jobs off your to do list and focus on the many more important things you have to do in the run up to your baby's birth and in the first few weeks afterwards. The knowledge that you are organised and prepared is soothing and will help make your life pre and post birth simpler, calmer and less stressful.

Key Points From this Chapter

- Set it and forget it – bulk buying or pre-ordering means one less job for you to do in the future

- Get up to date with veterinary and grooming appointments etc

- Have a plan for your dog's care when you go into labour or are in hospital (and a Plan B!)

CHAPTER 10

GETTING TO KNOW YOU:

A PROCESS NOT AN EVENT

"A goal without a plan is just a wish"

Antoine de Saint Exupéry

In this chapter we are going to think about the most common question I am asked by expectant parents, "What is the best way to introduce my dog and my baby?". Introductions are, understandably, often at the forefront of expectant parents' minds but we'll consider whether this is the right question to ask and whether a different mindset might serve us better. We'll consider how you would like your dog to behave around your baby and what you can do to maximise your chances of success in achieving those goals. As we've learned previously taking the time to plan ahead can remove a lot of stress and help you feel more prepared and confident. Time spent planning is rarely wasted!

"How soon should we introduce our baby to our dog?". "How do I introduce the dog and the baby?" "Should I bring the baby to the dog or the dog to the baby?". These are all questions I am asked frequently and my answer to those questions is "Let's ask different questions!".

Keep Your Eyes on the Prize

Bringing your baby home is an exciting time and you'll be so thrilled and delighted to be introducing your little one to your friends and family. Our dogs are family too and so our inclination may be to include them in these exciting first meetings too. For many people their dog has been their first 'baby' and so it's important to them emotionally to include their dog in the joy of bringing their new baby home for the first time. These emotions are normal and entirely understandable. But let's step back and take a little bit of the emotion out of it, just for a moment, to consider what you want to achieve in the longer term and how you ultimately want your dog to behave around your baby. Is your aim to encourage interaction? Do you want to encourage proximity? Do you want to suggest to your dog that he should be interested in the baby? The answer to those questions is, no...these are not the behaviours that are likely to be helpful in the longer term.

Instead, what will make your life easier, calmer and less stressful is a dog who is largely disinterested in your baby and who displays calm, neutral and detached behaviours around them. Teaching your dog that the baby is of no particular interest or relevance to him is what will help you achieve that goal.

When we think of things in this way we can see that an excited, formal "introduction" where we encourage interest, proximity and engagement and generally create a "buzz" around the baby may be counterproductive and send mixed messages to your dog. It becomes confusing to your dog if interaction is encouraged in some circumstances but then discouraged in others and it is that confusion which can lead to your dog making the wrong choices.

Instead of focusing on the first step in the journey – the initial introduction – think about the ultimate destination – your dog becoming accustomed to your baby. While an introduction is a one off, and potentially exciting, event, habituation is a process which occurs over time. There is no need to rush that process and it is almost always better to expose your dog to your baby slowly and gently.

First Days

So, how do you plan your return home from hospital in a way that will encourage the behaviours you want from your dog?

I normally suggest that dad, or a friend if you are a lone parent, holds the baby as you enter the home to allow mum to safely greet the dog. If your dog is likely to jump up on you then it would be sensible to consider how you might handle that if you are recovering from a caesarean section or are feeling physically fragile or sore. Having a friend or family member there to hold the dog on lead in order to prevent them being able to jump can be very helpful.

Then try and keep your behaviour as normal and unremarkable as possible. Make a cup of tea, settle down on the couch and relax. One parent can sit with the baby while one sits with the dog, still on lead, at a slight distance allowing him to simply observe from a distance. Reward him well with a high value treat (have these prepared beforehand) for any calm behaviours he offers. If he sits, lies down, settles or even just looks away from the baby reward him for that. What gets rewarded gets repeated so rewarding these calm, disinterested behaviours means that your dog will be more likely to repeat them again in the future. You could encourage these settled behaviours whilst also redirecting your dog's attention away from the baby by giving him a stuffed food toy like a KONG ™ or a tasty chew. When you are happy that your dog is calm and relaxed you may allow your dog to approach the baby, still on lead, and have a sniff of your baby's feet – not your baby's head or nappy area - if he wants to. Only allow him to approach if he is calm and never cajole him or lure him with treats if he is hesitant or uncertain about the baby. Keep the interaction brief, calm and low key and then redirect your dog to another fun activity like a chew or a KONG or going out for a walk. Remember – there is no need to rush this process. If you need to take a few days before you feel confident allowing your dog to approach the baby that is absolutely fine. It's always better to go slowly than to rush things unnecessarily.

If Your Dog is Worried

Think back for a moment to the chapter on body language, in particular the signs of anxiety or stress.

If your dog displays any of these signs in the presence of the baby then the first and most important thing to do is increase the distance between them. This might mean removing him to another room, taking him out to the garden for a sniff or a play or taking him out for a walk. Allow him a break, a chance to decompress, and then try bringing him into the same room as the baby again later.

Remember (again!), there's no rush. It's so important to listen to what your dog is telling you and move forward at his pace. Never feel tempted to lure him closer to the baby with treats. Trying to speed up the process runs the risk of backfiring and creating yet more stress and anxiety. Instead, moving at his pace, rewarding any calm and relaxed behaviours he offers and giving him the time and space to observe and assess at a distance where he feels comfortable is far more likely to reduce his anxiety and help him feel more comfortable around the baby.

Supervision

It goes without saying that full active, adult supervision is required at all times when dogs and children are together. If both parents are in the room one can be on 'baby duty' and one on 'dog duty'. If only one parent is around then using crates, tethers or baby gates to create some physical separation is a sensible precaution. We'll discuss the importance of supervision and separation more fully in the next chapter.

Bringing Home a Blanket

If you go to any search engine and enter the search term "introducing a dog and a baby" one piece of advice is almost ubiquitous.... sending home a blanket with the baby's scent on for the dog to sniff.

The theory behind the advice is that familiarising your dog to your baby's scent prior to meeting the baby will allow the dog to recognise the baby and will also create a positive association with the baby in the dog's mind. Now, this sounds ok in theory but let's think about this a little more.

Imagine you have invited a new friend to your home for dinner. Do you ask them to submit a piece of clothing first so that your dog can familiarise himself with their scent? No! Of course you don't. So, if we don't do this for other new people our dog meets is there any logical reason to do so when we are bringing a baby home for the first time?

Secondly, can exposure to a particular scent create a positive association? Yes, it can BUT, generally, that exposure has to happen multiple times while being paired with good things, like treats, in order to create a strong positive emotional response. A one-time exposure to a scent is highly unlikely to result in any association being made by your dog, positive or otherwise.

In chapter one we discussed the incredible power of a dog's nose. When we consider that a dog is capable of detecting subtle changes in our body chemistry it seems theoretically possible, at least, that they can smell a 7lb human being! So perhaps your dog is already familiar with your baby's scent? I'm not aware of any evidence for this but it's an interesting point to ponder.

The prevalence of this advice, almost to the exclusion of anything else, runs the risk of lulling parents into a false sense of security. There's a risk that parents believe that because they have done this one thing they've done everything they need to. But, as you are learning in this book there is a lot more to preparing your dog for life with a baby than simply smelling a blanket.

Will sending home a blanket for your dog to sniff do any harm if you are also taking the other steps outlined in this book? No, I don't believe so. But I don't believe it will do any good either. And that is another reason that I don't recommend bringing home a blanket. The bottom line is that you will have enough on your plate at that particular time in your life. The first days of your baby's life are a roller coaster. You are likely tired, busy, probably quite stressed and a bit overwhelmed at becoming new parents. You want to be focusing your energies on caring for your new baby and on the things that you need to do, not on things that are unlikely to be of any benefit to you.

Summary

When you first have your dog and your new baby in the same space it can be understandably tempting to rush to introduce them immediately. In fact, it's a question many people will ask you... "How did the dog react?".

However remember what your ultimate goal is – a dog who is comfortable around your baby but largely disinterested. Keeping that in mind will help you reframe that first interaction as the first step in an ongoing process rather than a one time, make or break introduction. Take the pressure off yourself, take the pressure of your dog and just go slowly. Less is more.

Key Points From This Chapter

- It's a process, not an event!

- Take your time...there is no rush

- Aim for calm, disinterest from your dog

- Reward your dog generously for the behaviour you want

- Move at your dog's pace

- Concentrate your efforts on things that will make a real difference

CHAPTER 11

THE KEYS TO SAFETY: SUPERVISION AND SEPARATION

"Safety doesn't happen by accident"

Anonymous

The number one priority for any new parents is keeping their child safe. The primal, instinctive protectiveness a new parent feels for their child overrides everything else. The presence of a dog in your home means that safety is even more at the forefront of a new parent's mind. It's important to remember that every dog has the potential to cause harm regardless of temperament or breed and we should never leave things to chance or become complacent regardless of how 'bulletproof' we think our dogs are.

There are two elements to keeping children safe around dogs – an understanding of canine body language and supervision. We have already learned how to listen to what our dogs are telling us with their body language and how to spot the subtle signals that they may be uncomfortable or worried by a situation. In this chapter we are going to consider the role supervision and separation play in creating a safe environment for your dog and your baby.

One of the primary goals of this book is to enable the inclusion of your dog in family life in a safe and appropriate way. We don't want to have to separate our dogs constantly from the rest of the family. They are part of our family, after all. Appropriate supervision, along with the judicious use of physical separation, allows your dog to be safely included in family life. This inclusion allows them to become habituated to the sights and sounds of your baby and gives us the opportunity to reward any appropriate behaviour offered in your baby's presence. You can't teach your dog how to behave around your child if they are constantly separated.

Family Paws ® Parent Education is an organisation devoted to providing support and education for families with dogs and they have many fabulous resources available to parents (further details can be found in Appendix B Further Resources). Family Paws ® have created a clear and helpful way to think about supervision which identifies five key concepts. They are –

- **Absent Supervision** – no adult supervision

- **Passive Supervision** – an adult is present but is distracted or not paying attention

- **Reactive Supervision** – an adult is supervising but waits until intervention is needed before acting

- **Proactive Supervision** – an adult has taken proactive, practical steps to set up the environment to keep dog and child apart

- **Active Supervision** – full adult, awake, active supervision with 100% of your focus and attention on both the child and the dog

Let's consider each of these in a little more detail.

Absent Supervision

Everyone knows that young children and dogs should never be left unsupervised. That goes without saying. It's the number one rule in keeping dogs and children safe. However, while the vast majority of responsible adults would never intentionally leave a dog and baby unsupervised, absent supervision can happen accidentally. For example the baby is asleep in their nursery and the door has been left open allowing the dog access. Perhaps the most common accidental reason for absent supervision is the supervising adult falling asleep. New parents are sleep deprived and mums may also be recovering physically from the birth adding to levels of fatigue. If you are resting on the sofa or sitting in a chair feeding your baby it is all too easy to find yourself falling asleep. I remember often falling asleep myself when I was sitting feeding my daughters. Sitting in a comfortable chair, warm, relaxed, with a baby in your arms feeding is soothing and peaceful. If you are breastfeeding the release of hormones oxytocin and prolactin can also induce relaxation and sleep. Be aware of the risk and if you feel you might be at risk of dozing off put the dog in another room or in their crate. If your baby is asleep away from you make sure your dog can't access their nursery.

Passive Supervision

Passive supervision occurs when there is an adult in the room but they are distracted by another activity which diverts their attention away from the child and the dog. It's happened to us all – your phone rings, or there's a knock at the door, or you are involved in another task like preparing food or answering an email. A recent study showed that the average smartphone user receives over sixty notifications daily so it's hardly surprising our attention sometimes wanders. The key, again, is to be aware of the risk. If something occurs which requires your attention take proactive steps to separate your dog and baby before you deal with it.

Reactive Supervision

Reactive supervision occurs when an adult is

supervising the interaction between child and dog but intervenes only when something is already happening which needs to be interrupted. For example, your baby begins to crawl towards your dog and gets a little too close and only then do you rush in and stop it. Or your dog approaches your baby who is lying in his bouncer and you call him away when he gets too close. Our reactions to those events are often sudden, loud and harsh in tone which has the potential to create negative associations about the proximity of your child for your dog.

Proactive Supervision

Proactive supervision happens when the supervising adult has taken steps in advance to ensure the safety of both child and dog by creating some physical separation. If you want to settle down and read a book or watch television while your baby plays under their baby gym then be proactive by settling your dog in another room, behind a gate or in his crate with a chew or a stuffed KONG ™. A proactive parent takes steps, in advance, to ensure that physical barriers are in place to avoid any unintentional interactions.

Active Supervision

Full, adult, awake, active supervision means that 100% of your focus and attention is on your dog and your child 100% of the time. You are actively involved in their interaction, not merely observing from a distance. This is the gold standard of supervision.

Make Active and Proactive supervision your goal and aim to avoid Absent, Passive and Reactive supervision.

Success Stations

Maintaining active supervision requires focus and concentration. It can be draining to keep up for long periods and, sometimes, it's just not possible. We all have meals to cook, phone calls to make, chores to do and books to read which mean that we can't devote 100% of our focus and attention solely on our dogs and children.

This is where proactive control and management techniques come in. 'Control and management' in dog training parlance simply means arranging the environment to prevent dogs performing behaviours we don't want. We may not be actively teaching them something but we are preventing them getting things wrong.

A Success Station is the Family Paws ® term for a safe and comfortable space where a dog will not have access to the baby. The dog has been set up to succeed because he can't get it 'wrong'. We can use baby gates, crates or pens to create success stations and we'll consider the pros and cons of these later.

A success station should always be a positive place for your dog. They should be introduced gradually and never used for extended periods. It may well be a new experience for your dog to be able to see you but be unable to reach you so begin to introduce these well in advance of when you need to use them.

Success stations can be created using –

- Tethers

- Crates

- Baby gates

Tethers

A tether anchored to a piece of heavy furniture can create separation without a physical barrier.

Tethers can be particularly useful during the early days as they allow your dog to observe safely from a distance without the risk of him being able to reach your baby. It allows your dog to move around within the boundary of the tether and offers less restriction than a crate or a pen might do. During the initial days of having a dog and baby together in the same room they can also help parents feel more confident and relaxed.

Tethers are not a replacement for adult supervision and they are only suitable for use with immobile babies. Once your baby begins to roll or crawl then tethers are no longer a suitable method of separation since they restrict your dog's ability to move away from or escape an approaching child. A tethered dog should never be left alone in case of accidents or entanglements.

Crates

A crate should always be a positive place for your dog, never a place of punishment or banishment. It should be a safe, secure place which your dog associates with good things and where he knows he will be left in peace. As with any piece of equipment it should be introduced positively and gradually. If your dog has not previously been crate trained then start working on that now if you intend to use a crate as a success station. There are some simple crate training notes in Appendix A to get you started. Remember we are aiming for inclusion so the crate should be located somewhere that allows your dog still to observe family life around them.

The downsides of a crate are that they very much limit your dog's freedom of movement so shouldn't be used for extended periods. They can also take up a significant amount of floorspace so may not be suitable for every home.

Baby Gates

These are hugely useful pieces of equipment in any home containing both young children and dogs. They can be used to create dog-free zones, for example, many people have one across the bottom of the stairs to restrict the dog's access to the upper floors. Baby gates allow your dog significant freedom of movement and allow them to observe family life rather than being shut away behind a solid door. There are many different styles of baby gates, some more robust and secure than others. If you have a strong or boisterous dog make sure you choose a style which he won't be able to bulldoze through! One other downside of gates, for some dogs, is that they can be jumpable.

Acclimatising your dog to as many of these success stations as possible gives you a range of practical options at your disposal to create the separation you need to go about family life safely and ensure adequate and appropriate separation. As your baby develops and grows some options will become more or less suitable and you may have to change your approach. For example you may need two layers of separation between an inquisitive toddler and a dog resting in his crate.

Summary

Along with an understanding of body language, the cornerstones of safety for children and dogs are supervision and separation. Being aware of the different kinds of supervision will help you ensure that you always have in place proactive or active supervision. Success stations are safe, comfortable, positive places which keep your dog physically separate from your child, thereby keeping them successful. Think about which options will best suit your dog and your lifestyle and begin to introduce them now.

Key Points From This Chapter

- Supervision and separation are fundamental in creating safe, harmonious environments for dogs and children

- Always aim for active or proactive supervision
- Use tethers, crates or baby gates to create success stations for your dog

CHAPTER 12

ENRICHMENT

In order to lead a fulfilled and satisfying life we need things that go beyond the basic fundamental needs of a roof over our head and enough food to eat. We need healthy relationships with our friends and loved ones, we need exercise. And beyond even those we need things which add value and enjoyment to our lives – films to watch, books to read, art to appreciate, music to listen to, games and puzzles to stimulate our minds. A life lacking those things would be impoverished indeed.

Our dogs are no different. In order to live their best life they need more than two walks a day and their dinner. They need a strong bond with their humans, they need interaction and they need opportunities to display natural behaviours and use their amazing abilities. They need enrichment.

Enrichment activities aim to increase the physical and psychological wellbeing of an animal by giving it opportunities to display natural behaviours. They are essential to the overall wellbeing of an animal. A dog who lives a satisfying, enriched life is far less likely to display problematic behaviours in the home. Rather than seeing enrichment as a "bonus" we should see it as a fundamental need which must always be met but even more so at a time when we are asking the dog to cope with decreased opportunities for stimulation in other areas of their lives.

Time is a scarce commodity when you have a new baby, and routines can be hard to establish and take a while to settle into. As we've learned, this often means that our dogs are likely to get less exercise than they have previously been used to and also, perhaps, reduced mental stimulation. An under stimulated dog with a lot of unspent physical energy may begin to display problematic behaviours as a result of either frustration or boredom, or a bit of both. They will seek out things to do which, while they may be rewarding for the dog, may be less rewarding for us, for example, barking at the window, chewing the furniture or seeking out constant attention from us.

We can help offset some of this reduction in physical exercise and reduce the chances of problem behaviours arising by offering our dogs constructive and interesting things to do instead. In short, by enriching their lives.

There are almost limitless ways to add enrichment into your dog's life. When considering the best choices for your dog it is a good idea to think about what they would choose to do left to their own devices. Does your dog love movement? Food? Sniffing? Digging? What brings your dog joy?

For the purposes of this book there is an additional important criterion for choosing suitable enrichment activities for your dog. Not only does your dog have to enjoy it but it has to be something that realistically fits into your busy life with a new baby. For example, a common enrichment activity is to stuff treats into toilet roll tubes and let your dog rip the tubes apart to find the treats. Great for your dog but leaves a lot of mess to clear up which is not what you want just now! Remember, we are trying to make your life easier as well as engaging your dog, so choose your activities wisely!

Many enrichment activities revolve around food. Our dogs have to eat and being creative about how we feed them gives us opportunities each day to add value and interest to their lives with the added bonus of keeping them constructively occupied for longer than the thirty seconds it takes for most dogs to eat their meals.

Scatter Feeding

Perhaps the simplest enrichment activity of all. Simply scatter your dog's food across a wide area and let them use their superpower, their sense of smell, to hunt for each piece of food. You can do this indoors or outdoors and incorporate it into your walks with your dog. I feed my own dog, Charlie, this way often. I scatter his food across the grass in the back garden and he spends ages searching out the food, his tail wagging constantly while he goes.

One thing I have noticed when I feed Charlie this way is that he continues sniffing round the garden long after the food has gone. The food is the initial reason to sniff but when it's gone he then finds other things of interest to investigate which keep him occupied and engaged for even longer.

Sniffing itself has other benefits for your dog. Studies have shown that sniffing lowers a dog's pulse and that the more engaged in the behaviour they are the greater the decrease in pulse rate. It is calming, self-soothing and is linked to the production of dopamine one of the chemicals in the brain associated with feelings of motivation and pleasure. A dog who sniffs is more likely to be an optimistic, satisfied, happy dog with a resultant positive impact on behaviour

KONGs ™

KONGs ™ are popular for a reason! Robust. Durable. A toy. An interactive feeder. They are a fantastic way to keep your dog entertained, enriched and occupied.

If your dog is new to KONGs ™ you should start by making access to the food really easy for your dog. Enrichment activities should involve some challenge but should never be frustrating. Start by adding just a few pieces of kibble (dry dog food pellets) or other dry treats which will fall out easily when your dog nudges the KONG ™. You want him to make the connection that food comes out of this toy! Then you can start to pack the KONG ™ a little more tightly to make the treats a little harder to extract. You can progress to freezing the KONG to make it harder still. Don't make it too challenging too quickly or you risk your dog becoming bored and giving up.

You can buy pre-prepared Kong fillers but these are expensive and it's simple to make your own fillings to suit your own dog. It doesn't need to take a huge amount of time and one parent can stuff a batch of KONGs ™ while the other parent is feeding the baby. Pop them in the freezer and you will have enrichment at your fingertips whenever you need it.

The possibilities are endless but here are some ideas to get you started.

Kibble – soak some of your dog's kibble in a little water or low salt stock until it softens a little then stuff into the Kong & freeze. Serve frozen to give your dog an extra challenge!

Canned Dog Food - super simple! You can add kibble and serve as it is or freeze

Peanut butter – just make sure it doesn't contain the artificial sweetener xylitol as that's toxic to dogs. You could also add some mashed banana

Banana – mashed banana is a hit with lots of dogs. For an extra antioxidant kick you could add some blueberries

Yoghurt – stuff the hole at the bottom with a piece of kibble or a little banana / strawberry, fill with natural yoghurt & freeze. You can also add chunks fruit like strawberries or banana to the yoghurt

Sweet Potato & Tuna – mash together and freeze. This also works well with sardines or mackerel or leftover mashed potato

Leftovers – makes good use of your leftovers. Combine mashed potato, left over vegetables, a little gravy…whatever you have!

Cream Cheese & Apple – combine soft cream cheese with diced apple & refrigerate or freeze.

Tuna – another super simple one. Stuff tuna (in water, not oil or brine) into the Kong & freeze

KONGs ™ give dogs an outlet for their natural licking and chewing behaviours and, in addition, will keep them occupied while you eat or feed the baby.

Note – KONGs ™ are very robust but if your dog is a power chewer you might want to consider the KONG ™ Extreme which is made of a tougher rubber and is (almost) indestructible.

Snuffle Mat

A snuffle mat looks a bit like a small, deep pile, shaggy rug. It consists of strips of fleece material tied to a rubber base. The strips form a deep pile in which tiny treats or pieces of kibble can nestle. If your dog is fed on kibble this is a wonderful way to feed them their daily rations. Scatter the kibble or treats over the mat and give it a gentle shake to help the food drop down deep into the pile. Your dog then has to use their nose to find and extract the pieces of food. As with scatter feeding this gives dogs the opportunity to use their dominant sense, scent, with all the benefits that that brings.

Puzzle Feeders

Puzzle feeders are toys which require dogs to use their nose or their paws or otherwise work and problem solve in order to access food. Puzzle feeders, and some other forms of enrichment, capitalise on a phenomenon known as contrafreeloading which means that, given a choice between 'free' food and food which has to be worked for, an organism will choose the food which requires effort.

There is a huge range of puzzle feeders on the market. Some of my favourites are produced by The KONG ™ Company, Nina Ottosson and K9 Connectables (you'll find links to all these companies in Appendix B Further Resources).

An important point to remember is that enrichment

activities should always be challenging but never frustrating. Feeding your dog entirely from challenging puzzle feeders may increase frustration so always observe your dog's behaviour. If they appear frustrated at any point give them an easier option.

Lickimat

A Lickimat is a small textured rubber mat; some have bristles, some have grooves, some have dimples. They can be spread with any wet food – raw food, wet dog food, peanut butter, yoghurt, cheese spread…anything spreadable. I suggest these be used as an extra treat or as a way of helping your dog soothe* rather than as a way of delivering a dog's main meal as I think, for some dogs there is a risk of frustration if they are hungry but the method of delivery means they can only access the food very slowly. While scatter feeding or a snuffle mat also slow the eating process down there is an element of searching and hunting involved in them which, as we've learned, increases levels of the feel good chemical, dopamine, making the experience more likely to be satisfying. Think of a lickimat as you might an ice cream cone or ice lolly…nice for a treat but you probably wouldn't want to eat your whole meal that way.

*Licking is one way in which dogs self soothe so a lickimat can be a useful way of helping your dog calm himself if he is showing signs of being anxious or worried.

Chews

Sniffing, licking and chewing are all activities which can calm and soothe dogs. Chewing also has the added bonus that it encourages a settled, lying down posture. Chewing is a natural canine behaviour and having a good selection of chews gives your dog a safe and appropriate outlet for that behaviour. The range of chews on the market is vast but my preference is for natural chews like antlers, pizzles or yak milk chews over those which have been chemically processed like rawhide.

There are also a number of ways to add enrichment into your dog's life which don't revolve around food.

Water

Many dogs LOVE water. If you have access to water whilst out for a walk with your dog why not stop there for a while and let him play in the water. Chasing stones, paddling or swimming all provide excellent physical exercise and add little variety into your dog's life. In summer months you could have a paddling pool in the garden for your dog to play in to provide some physical activity.

Digging

This is Charlie's favourite thing ever! Often on our walks he'll catch a scent and start to dig. This can keep him happily occupied and absorbed for a significant amount of time. If the weather is good I just find a comfortable spot, have a seat and let him get on with it. By the time he is finished he is physically tired (digging is hard physical work!) and mentally tired. After a digging session he always comes home and has a long sleep. To provide a suitable outlet for digging in the garden you could provide a sandpit for your dog or fence of an area of the garden where they are allowed to dig.

Toys

The pleasure dogs find in toys often comes from the fact that they get to interact with us whilst playing with them. The interaction is a fundamental part of the fun. This is why some dogs will rarely play with toys independently.

When you have a moment try to build a little play into your dog's day – throw the ball for him or have a game of tug – you'll be meeting his need for attention and interaction and thereby avoiding him seeking attention in other ways. One game with a toy that many dogs do love to do independently is to disembowel a stuffed toy. This can keep them happily absorbed for some time but the downside is you are left with the innards to tidy up! Whether the cost is worth the benefit will depend on how long the activity absorbs your dog for.

Sniffing

Allowing your dog the time to sniff when they are out on their walk is such an easy way to add so much enrichment and enjoyment into their day. Scent is your dog's primary sense – it's how they interpret the world around them. Not giving them time to sniff is like taking a human to an art gallery and not allowing them to look at the pictures.

When you go out for a walk move slowly, using as long a lead as you safely can for the environment you are in (a dog on a four foot lead can barely move from your side to find interesting scents) and if your dog finds a scent that interests him let him sniff for as long as he wants. Don't think of your walk as having to cover a certain distance, just meander together through the environment. It's more relaxing for you too – there's no rush to be anywhere, no hurry.

Your dog will find thirty minutes of a slow, sniffy walk just as satisfying, if not more so, as thirty minutes of fast paced exercise. They are also far more likely to settle after a low arousal activity like sniffing than a high arousal activity like ball chasing.

Summary

Enrichment activities allow a dog to display natural behaviours and are essential for a dog's physical and emotional wellbeing. They should form a part of every dog's life, every day. But they are even more crucial than normal at a time of significant change in a dog's life when they are likely to be getting less exercise and less attention.

Providing your dog with a variety of absorbing, thoughtful activities will help keep him fulfilled and satisfied and so reduce the risk of problematic behaviours arising. However, it is really important to remember that enrichment is not just about keeping your dog busy and out of your hair. Yes – it keeps them constructively employed at a time when you are busy but it goes deeper than that. It's about mindfully giving them the variety and enjoyment they need, and deserve, out of life.

Key Points From This Chapter

- Enrichment activities increase the physical and psychological wellbeing of an animal by giving it opportunities to display natural behaviours

- Offsetting a reduction in exercise and attention by increasing enrichment activities can help avoid problematic behaviours arising out of boredom or frustration

- Enrichment activities should feature in every dog's life, every day

CHAPTER 13

BE KIND TO YOURSELF: SELF CARE & SELF COMPASSION

"You can't pour from an empty cup"

Anonymous

At first glance self-care and self-compassion may seem like unconventional topics for a book about dogs or dog training. But the principle aim of this book isn't teaching you how to train your dog to perform specific behaviours; it is about helping you and your dog prepare for, and adapt to, a huge lifestyle change with as little stress as possible.

We've covered many ways to reduce potential stress for your dog but we also need to consider the human end of the lead. The expectations and pressure we put on ourselves can be hugely stressful and can taint our experiences of early parenthood. The fact you are reading this book shows that you are being considerate of your dog's experience. You also need to be considerate of your own.

From my own personal experience as a parent, and from working with many new and expectant parents, I think it's almost universal that we put huge pressure on ourselves to do everything perfectly, especially if we are first time parents. I haven't yet met parents who don't feel a huge weight of responsibility to protect and care for this precious, new, vulnerable infant. And if you are a dog owner with a new baby you are very likely to feel additional pressures and responsibilities. You are likely to be concerned about ensuring your baby's safety around your dog, you may feel apprehensive about how your dog is going to react to your baby, you may be worried about whether you are going to cope with the practicalities of managing a dog and a baby in the same home. Many dog owning parents also worry that they won't have sufficient time to be able to fulfil their much loved dog's needs adequately.

Well-meaning friends and family can add to your emotional burden when they question whether having a dog and a baby together is a good idea, or they continually tell you what hard work it will be or tell you that you're not going to be able to look after your dog properly once your baby is here.

In short there are lots of ways for us to put pressure on ourselves and lots of things for us to potentially worry about. And all of these come at a time when we are facing the huge challenges of preparing for parenthood and learning how to be a parent. It is sixteen years since my first daughter was born but, as I sit here and write this, I can still vividly remember holding her in my arms, looking down at her perfectness and wondering how on earth I was ever going to be able to nurture and care for this tiny baby. It was an overwhelming mixture of pure love for her and sheer terror that I might mess up this perfect little creature. She was hours old and I was already putting pressure on myself.

The media, and social media in particular, feeds us a constant diet of unattainable images. Perfect, beautiful, co-ordinated families with immaculate homes and enviable lifestyles. It is a fiction. Family life, particularly in the early days, is a messy, chaotic mix of tears and joy and poo and sick and being in your milk stained, mismatched pyjamas at 2 o'clock in the afternoon. It is not perfect. And it doesn't have to be. If you remember nothing else from this chapter remember that. Further, we shouldn't be trying to make it perfect (did I mention that's unattainable). Don't put yourself under that degree of pressure - it's not helpful to you in any way. It's just going to make you feel tense and stressed and anxious. It doesn't have to be perfect; it just has to be good enough.

Be kind to yourself. If you are having a difficult day

and your dog's walk is shorter than usual or is replaced by a snuffle and a play in the garden don't be hard on yourself about it. Instead of focusing on the missed walk remind yourself of all the preparation you have done up to this point to help your dog cope with exactly these situations. Dogs are adaptable and resilient beings and, within reason, they will cope with these disruptions to their normal routine especially if you have taken the time to prepare them in advance. If the house is calm and quiet with baby and dog both contented and asleep take that moment to relax and rest. Don't feel the need to rush to the next job on your to do list. Think about the advice you would give to a friend in your position and take it on board yourself.

Accept offers of help. When you have a new baby you get lots of offers of help from people. However, accepting that help, or asking for it, can be difficult and uncomfortable. It can create feelings of vulnerability and feel like an admission of failure or weakness. Even if you don't have negative feelings about accepting help it's instinctive in lots of us to turn down offers of help. We can all benefit from help sometimes so if you are offered help, take it! People love to feel wanted and will be delighted that you accepted their offer in the spirit it was made. Ask them to walk your dog; or ask them to care for your baby while you walk your dog. Allow someone to make you a cup of tea or fold your laundry. Knowing when to accept help is a sign of strength, not weakness.

Get outside. Dogs and babies are wonderful excuses (if you need one) to get outside. Being outdoors, especially in green spaces, is wonderfully beneficial. Multiple academic studies have all shown the same thing - time spent outdoors lowers blood pressure, reduces stress and improves our mood and mental health; particularly interesting for postpartum women it has also been shown to help us heal more quickly. I remember the first few times I was brave enough to attempt to go for a walk with my daughter and Syd, our dog. It felt like a military operation - getting my daughter dressed and into her snowsuit (she was a winter baby) was a job in itself! Then popping her back in her cot while I got the pram outside (whilst also keeping the dog inside). Settling the baby in the pram, going back into the house to collect the dog, managing the lead and the dog and the pram. The first few times were exhausting and some days it was tempting to take the easy option and just stay at home. But like anything else the routine became easier with practice and our time outside benefitted us all. I felt physically and mentally better, it gave me a feeling of competency and achievement, my dog was having his needs met and fresh air made my daughter sleep like a.... well, like a baby. Try to get out, if you can, every day, even if it is only for a short walk (always remembering the 'be kind to yourself' rule and not beating yourself up about it if there are days that you can't).

Get some alone time. Being a new mum is tough at times. It's relentless. Your baby's total dependence on you for everything, especially if you are breastfeeding, can be overwhelmingly exhausting and even claustrophobic at times. These feelings are normal and shouldn't be ignored. For your own wellbeing and sense of identity it's really important to ensure you get adequate time alone. Go for a long shower or a soak in the bath. While your partner goes out with the baby make yourself a cup of tea and enjoy it in peace. If you are able, try occasionally to go for a walk alone with your dog. Being out in the fresh air on your own, with your dog is a wonderful respite from the relentlessness that is being a new mum. And your dog will love the connection and attention too. Mums often feel guilty for needing a break but it's essential for your own wellbeing and to remind you that you are still you, not 'just' a mum.

Hang out with your dog. You might have read about the role of the hormone oxytocin in mother/child bonding. Eye contact between a mother and her baby increases the amount of oxytocin in the mother's body resulting in an increase in maternal behaviours and emotional bonding with their baby who in turn become more closely attached to their mother which increases her oxytocin levels still further driving more nurturing behaviour and so on. It becomes a virtuous cycle. The hormone also plays a crucial role in romantic love. In short oxytocin is involved in feelings of attachment and love. When we pet our dog the level of the oxytocin increases both in our body and in our dog's. It is oxytocin which gives rise to the deep feelings of attachment and bonding that we experience with our dogs. The arrival of a new baby inevitably means we spend less time with our dogs but finding a little time devoted just to being with them will keep your bond strong while reducing stress levels and aiding overall wellbeing for both of you.

Summary

Being a new parent is hard. Being a new parent with a dog adds an extra layer of complexity and effort to an already hard job. It's only fair to yourself that you try to treat yourself with as much thought, compassion and kindness as you treat your dog.

I'm not counsellor or a self-help expert but I am a parent and I remember well the pressure I needlessly put myself under to do everything perfectly. As a trainer working with expectant families I have often seen the relief on their faces when I tell them that their dog's world won't end if they miss a walk occasionally. Giving people permission not to have to be perfect is liberating for them.

Aiming for good enough instead of perfect and being kind to yourself will make the early days of parenthood much less stressful and more enjoyable.

Key Points From This Chapter

- It doesn't have to be perfect

- Be kind to yourself

- Accept offers of help

- Get some alone time

- Hang out with your dog

CHAPTER 14

WHEN THINGS GO WRONG

Sometimes things go wrong. Sometimes things don't go to plan. Sometimes life throws us a curve ball which changes everything for us. Despite our best laid plans and our detailed preparations we find ourselves in the situation we never hoped to be in – wondering if we can keep our dog in our home.

There are a variety of reasons why we might find ourselves in that position. Perhaps a failure of supervision or separation lead to an incident which worried or scared you? Perhaps your health or the health of your child have impacted your ability to care for your dog as you would like? Perhaps you have found parenthood and the demands it brings just too overwhelming and you have no energy or time left for your dog? Perhaps, despite the work you've done, your dog is finding it hard to cope in a home with a baby?

Let's consider some of the reasons owners might find themselves having to consider whether they can keep their dog in their home.

An Incidence of Aggression

Before we consider what your longer term response to an incidence of aggression might be let's stop and consider what you should do in the moment.

Hearing your dog growl at your child is a heart stopping moment for any parent. Your reaction may well be to panic, punish the dog and immediately start to consider options like re-homing. But stop...breathe...it may not be as bad as you think.

So what should you do? Firstly, calmly separate your dog and your baby. Either by calling the dog to you or by calmly removing your baby. If at all possible try to avoid lifting or physically moving your dog or you could risk a bite yourself.

Secondly, don't punish your dog for growling. Does this sound like crazy advice? Surely he needs to learn that growling at children is wrong? But all behaviour happens for a reason and growling is no different. A growl is an early warning system which tells you that, in that moment, your dog is uncomfortable or anxious about the presence or behaviour of your baby. His growl gives us an opportunity to intervene and defuse the situation before things escalate. If the dog is punished for growling we run the risk, not only of disabling that early warning system, but also of creating further negative associations with the baby.

Try to identify the triggers. What was happening just before the growl? Was your baby crying? Did they startle or make some other movement? Did you move towards the dog while holding the baby? Was the dog sleeping? Eating? Playing with a toy? If you understand the triggers then you are more likely to be able to predict, and so, prevent the same situation happening in the future.

Increase supervision. Was your attention momentarily diverted and you missed a warning sign from your dog that they were becoming uncomfortable? It happens to the best of us. Active supervision of children and dogs is essential to keep everyone safe and happy. If you can't supervise, separate.

After you have dealt with the immediate aftermath of an aggressive incident you need to take a step back, take a breath and calmly consider what happened, what went wrong and whether (and how) you can change things in the future to avoid a repetition of the incident. In many cases it is often an unfortunate series of events which resulted in the incident and with a few adjustments to supervision and separation any repetition can be successfully avoided in the future.

Seek help from a qualified dog professional, ideally with experience of dog/child dynamics such as a Family Paws Parent Educator. They will be able to help you identify what went wrong and work with you to minimise the chance of any repetition.

Whether or not a single incident is severe enough or has damaged your confidence enough for you to feel that your dog cannot stay in the family will depend on the individual circumstances of the case and is a decision only you can make. The important thing is to make it with a clear head and not in a moment of panic.

Health and Wellbeing

We all hope for an easy birth, a quick recovery and a healthy child but sadly that is not always the case. Postnatal illness or the diagnosis of disability or illness in the baby can have a devastating impact on family life and on our relationships with our companion animals.

Postnatal depression is estimated to affect up to one in ten women within the first year of their baby's life. In addition to persistent sadness or low mood some women may also experience feelings of anger or resentment towards family members, including their dog. Women report feeling anger or irritation every time the dog makes a noise, moves or seeks attention; followed by guilt at the anger directed at their previously much loved dog. Their relationship with their pet becomes strained and tense. Even without these negative feelings towards the dog some women simply feel that the pressure of caring for their dog whilst ill is just too great.

Postnatal depression is treatable and as your health improves your relationship with your dog will improve so it's important not to make any impulsive or rash decisions. A decision to rehome may be a permanent solution to a temporary problem. Seek help at an early stage from your midwife or an organisation like Postpartum Support International (see the Further Resources section for contact details).

Even if you are not suffering from diagnosed postnatal depression you may still feel overwhelmed and out of your depth in the first weeks and months of parenthood. You may feel resentful of the additional work your dog brings or simply unable to fulfil his needs adequately. Feelings of guilt and failure may lead you to feel that you can't cope with both your dog and your baby.

These feelings are normal but, in most cases, they won't last forever. It can take time to find your rhythm and confidence as a parent but you almost certainly will.

How can you ride the wave of these temporary feelings of overwhelm or depression? Here are some suggestions –

- Get help – do you have a family member or friend who could walk your dog, or help with your laundry or run some errands for you? Could your dog go to stay with a family member or friend for a short period? Sometimes a few days respite can be enough to help you rest and re-group and feel able to cope more easily

- Use a dog walker or dog day care – take the pressure off yourself and outsource some of the tasks you are struggling to cope with

- Be kind to yourself – don't set your bar too high. Revisit the previous chapter and remember that things don't have to be perfect. If your baby is quiet and your dog is settled give yourself a break. Use that time to rest and have a cup of tea. The laundry can wait.

A child born with additional needs may require all of their parents' time and care, leaving nothing left for the family dog. This is a heart breaking situation for a family to find itself in and, thankfully, one that is rare. Whether you can realistically meet your dog's needs whilst caring for an ill or disabled child will depend on your own individual circumstances and support network. Caring adequately for a dog is undeniably another call on your time and one that you may not be able to fulfil. However dogs are wonderfully therapeutic and having another focus may offer you some respite from other caring responsibilities. The key advice I can offer here is, again, not to make snap decisions in the heat of emotion and to be realistic about whether you can find long term solutions to the new challenges you now face.

Your Dog

You have prepared as much as possible, you have introduced changes gently and gradually, you have given your dog the time and space to get used to your new arrival. You have done everything you could possibly have done and, yet your dog is struggling to cope living in a home with a baby. They may display highly aroused or predatory behaviour or fearful, anxious behaviour around the baby.

The steps outlined in this book are sound and in the vast majority of cases will help your dog cope more calmly with the arrival of a baby in their life.

However there are no guarantees. Dogs are living, breathing, sentient individuals who experience emotions in the same way we do.

It's an undeniable fact that some dogs cannot live safe, happy lives in close proximity to babies and children. Whether children trigger predatory instincts or whether they are fearful of children both of these situations are potentially dangerous for your child and stressful for your dog.

Are there ways to manage children and dogs if you find yourself in that situation? Potentially, yes. You could live in a gated community keeping children and dog separated by baby gates, crates or pens at all times. But management fails. One day someone will forget to shut a gate or your dog will escape from his crate. The potential for an accident is always there. Living under those conditions, having to be constantly vigilant, always on alert and unable to relax is a stressful way to live.

Your child's safety is obviously your main priority but also stop and consider your dog's welfare. Imagine a dog who is fearful or worried by children. Who growls if the child gets too close, who feels anxious or stressed simply by the presence of the child. Imagine living 24 hours a day, 7 days a week, 365 days a year in the same home as someone who scared you to that extent. That would be a hard, chronically stressful existence with little quality of life.

Making the decision to re-home under those circumstances is incredibly difficult for families. They can feel huge guilt that they have let their dog down. They often search for the 'magic wand' that will make everything ok. But some dogs will simply never be safe or happy living with children. In those cases it is the right decision for everyone – humans and dogs – to find the dog a child free home where he is able to live a more relaxed, less stressful life.

Summary

Sometimes things go wrong or don't turn out as planned. We make mistakes or misjudge a situation or are suddenly confronted with things outwith our control which move the goalposts.

In a book like this it could be tempting to gloss over the possibility that you will hit obstacles that appear to be, or in some cases are, insurmountable. But that's not the reality. It's important to acknowledge that sometimes we find ourselves having to consider tough choices. What I hope you have learned from this chapter is the importance of making decisions with a cool head and of being realistic about what is, and isn't, viable, or fair, in the long term.

Key Points From This Chapter

- There are no guarantees

- Learn from mistakes

- Don't rush into snap decisions in the heat of emotion
- Consider whether the issues you are facing are likely to be temporary or permanent

- Sometimes the hard decision is the right one for everyone – human and dog

CHAPTER 15

SOME COMMON QUESTIONS

What is the best way to introduce our baby to our dog?

Bringing your new baby home is such a thrilling time. You'll be so excited to introduce your baby to family and friends and so it's understandable you're keen for your dog to meet the baby too. It's worth thinking through what we want to achieve longer term and how we ultimately want the dog to interact with the baby. Do we want the dog to be really interested in the baby? To try to get near the baby or be hyper vigilant around the baby? Probably not… Ideally, we want the dog to ignore the baby and to learn that the baby isn't really relevant to him. So my advice would be that it's best not to make a big event out of returning home with your new baby…at least as far as your dog is concerned! In fact, aim to make it a bit of a non-event…. just business as usual. No excited introductions or up close encounters. We don't really want to encourage the dog to think the baby is something for him to be interested in or concerned about. I'd suggest keeping it all very low key and pretty uninteresting from the word go in order to give your dog good, clear information that the baby isn't his concern.

For more detailed information on this topic please see Chapter 10.

My dog is 5 years old and has never settled sleeping alone so he sleeps in my room with me. I guess it's not safe for that to continue but I'm not sure how to start to change that.

You are absolutely right that having a free roaming dog and a newborn in the same room while you sleep isn't safe. You won't be able to adequately supervise your dog as you'll also be asleep (at least some of the time, hopefully!). It's possible that a sudden cry or movement, like the startle reflex, might scare the dogs and result in unwanted behaviour. Your dog may roll over in the night and inadvertently harm your baby. Similarly, sitting in bed feeding your baby with a dog on the bed alongside you may make adequate supervision difficult. Let's think about the size of your dog.... would he be able to jump up to reach a cradle or cot? If your dog is small enough that he couldn't independently access either your bed or the crib then you may be able to keep him in your room but perhaps sleeping on a dog bed on the floor or in a crate. If your dog could potentially reach your baby then I'd recommend either having him sleep in a crate or teaching him to sleep outwith your room at least while the baby is sleeping alongside you. The important thing is to consider, objectively and honestly, what access your dog could gain to the baby when you are all sleeping in the same space and then make any changes necessary to prevent that access. Start to introduce those changes well in advance of your baby's due date so that your new bedtime routine is well established by the time baby is here to minimise any disruption to your precious sleep. And remember nothing is forever...if you decide that it would be safer to have your dog sleeping elsewhere initially you can always invite him back into your room when the baby has moved to his/her nursery.

For more information on introducing changes and supervision see Chapters 3 and 11.

Our dog currently has free rein to go wherever he pleases in the house but after our baby is born we don't want him to go upstairs. Should we start to restrict his access now?

Absolutely! That's a fabulous idea and great forward planning. Thinking about what areas you might want to restrict your dog's access to at this stage allows you work out the logistics of doing so – baby gates, locks, latches etc – while you have plenty of time. It will let you see the day to day practicalities of dog free zones and help you work out what works and what doesn't. And it also gives you time to help your dog with the transition by training any new behaviours necessary and getting him used to the new arrangements long before the baby arrives. By working on this in advance your dog will be well used to the changes by the time the baby arrives and it will also make the change unrelated to the new baby (from the dog's point of view). It will inevitably be a time of huge change for your dog and so any changes you can make in advance to minimise stress in the early days can only be beneficial.

For more information on introducing changes see Chapter 3.

My dog jumps up a lot and a friend has advised me to spray him in the face with water whenever he does this. Will this work to stop the jumping?

Jumping can be a real problem.... especially if you are holding a young baby in your arms. It's dangerous and he could harm the baby, albeit accidentally. However, aversive tools like water sprays aren't tools that I would recommend. While they can work to stop behaviour like jumping up they don't come without risks. The reason things like water sprays can work is because they are unpleasant for the dog and so the dog will try to avoid the spray by stopping jumping. However, it's not possible for us to control the associations the dog makes when the spray occurs and therein lies the problem. It is possible that your dog may come to associate the spray with the baby itself. This runs the risk that your dog becomes uncertain or fearful around your baby which could cause you difficulties in the longer term. Similarly, if your dog comes to associate you with unpleasant or painful consequences their trust in you may diminish and one of the keys to a confident, relaxed, happy dog is trust in his caregivers.

There are many more positive ways we could tackle the jumping up without those risks. For example, keeping your dog on lead or behind a baby gate and teaching him kindly to keep four paws on the ground.

For more information on teaching your dog new behaviours see Chapter 5.

How do I ensure that my dog and my baby become best friends?

It really is fantastic to see a strong bond developing between a dog and a child, isn't it? A happy, respectful relationship between our dogs and our children is what we all strive for. But it's important that we don't put too many expectations on our dogs to play a certain role in the relationship. We have to allow them to just be a dog without putting any pressure on them to be either a friend or a protector. Ideally, we want the baby to be largely irrelevant to your dog at this stage. The arrival of a new baby is a time of huge change for the whole family, including your dog, and we want him to feel happy and secure that you have things under control and that the new arrival is none of his concern. That's the scenario that will best set you all up for success.

For more information on why a gradual 'getting to know you' process is better than an expectation laden introduction see Chapter 10.

Are some breeds safer around children than others?

It's not unusual for people to have preconceptions that certain breeds are safer than others around children and it is important to consider breed traits but, in truth, all dogs have the potential for harm whether they are a pit bull or a miniature poodle. The crucial factors in keeping dog/child interactions safe and appropriate are an understanding of your individual dog, adequate supervision and being able to read your dog's body language.

These don't change regardless of breed. The important thing is to consider how best to create a safe, responsible environment for your new baby.

How do I make sure my dog understands that my baby is above him in the pack?

You don't! The concept of "pack theory" asserts that dogs live in a rigid hierarchy with an 'alpha' top dog who exerts dominance over subordinate members. This theory was very popular at one stage and is still very prevalent. However this theory has been proven to be false (in fact the scientist who first proposed it has since renounced it). Your dog knows that you and your baby are not dogs so acting as 'pack leader' will have no relevance to him at all. Rank and hierarchy are not things you need to worry about!

My midwife said we should bring home the baby blanket from the hospital and let the dog sniff it to help him accept the baby. Is this a good idea?

This is a really common suggestion and something that you'll probably hear often. But, in fact, a single exposure to the baby's scent is unlikely to make any real difference to the way your dog will feel about your baby. We don't take this approach with any other person we introduce to the dog so, if you think about it and it doesn't really make much sense doing it for a baby! It's unlikely to do any harm but similarly it's unlikely to do much good so, at a time in your life when you really have your hands full, I wouldn't bother!

For more information on this topic see Chapter 10.

I'm worried that I'm not going to have enough time to exercise or play with my dog as much as he's used to and that he might become bored. Do you have any suggestions?

You're right - you *will* have less time for your dog once your baby is here, particularly in the first few weeks and months. Try not to beat yourself up about it! It's inevitable but there are some simple things you can do to help minimise the impact on your dog. In the weeks running up to the birth of your baby reduce his exercise a little and vary it to begin to reflect how things might change after your baby is here. That might mean more on lead walks around the streets and less off lead walks through the fields. Making the changes gradual means that your dog has time to adapt. You might also want to consider employing a dog walker, if you don't already have one. Even if they only go out for one walk each week it means that you can relax in the knowledge that your dog is getting some good exercise. And you get some time off from juggling both dog and baby! Encourage him to begin settling alone some of the time. Settle him with a good chew or stuffed KONG ™ in one room while you catch up on some chores in another (or better yet, go and enjoy a relaxing bath!). If your dog is particularly attached to mum then encourage other family members to take over some of the doggy duties in the weeks before baby is due. You can make up for a reduction in physical exercise by replacing that with some simple enrichment activities which will keep your dog both mentally engaged and occupied. These needn't be fancy and can be as simple as scattering some treats or kibble over the garden for your dog to sniff out and find.

My dog has growled at children in the past. How do I make sure he doesn't do this to my baby?

If you know that your dog is uncertain around children then you *must* seek experienced, qualified, professional help as a matter of urgency. Look for a reward-based trainer in your local area to assist and guide you.

For more related information see Chapters 2, 4 and 11.

CHAPTER 16

FINAL THOUGHTS

You are about to embark on a new and exciting chapter in your life. You will have a vision of how life as a family will look and, more specifically, how life as a family with a dog will look. It's natural to hope for, expect even, a harmonious, happy household where your dog and your child co-exist happily and safely. And when it happens it is joyful. Children who are lucky enough to grow up with a happy, relaxed family dog are truly blessed. They have a loyal friend who will teach them so much about empathy, trust, respect and understanding.

Sometimes we are lucky and have a dog who will be that beloved, gentle friend to our children with little effort on our part. But, by being proactive, we can stack the deck in our favour and make that hoped for outcome less reliant on sheer luck.

In the introduction to this book I wrote that the arrival of a new baby is one of the most common reasons that dogs are surrendered for rehoming. As we've learned sometimes that decision to rehome is the right one perhaps because the dog is displaying serious behavioural issues which new parents haven't the resources to tackle safely or effectively, or because the dog is too stressed by the baby to have any quality of life in a home with children. Those cases are, thankfully, rare. However, more often, it is a combination of relatively low level problems coming to light at a time when new parents are exhausted and busy that lead people to make the decision that they can no longer keep their dog in their home. A horrible 'perfect storm' made even worse by the fact that many issues are avoidable with just a little work in advance.

Following the steps outlined in this book will go a long way to helping you avoid being in that heart breaking predicament. Rather than expecting your dog to cope with myriad changes over night – how much exercise they get, how much attention they get, where they sleep, strange sounds, new objects, perhaps being corrected or told off for behaviours that they have always done etc – the approach outlined here will ensure that these changes have been introduced well before your baby arrives. By that time they will be normal for your dog and any teething problems will be a distant memory. Less stress for your dog means less stress for you which can only be a good thing for everyone.

And not only will your dog be better prepared so will you. You will understand better who your dog is and how they react to things which stands you in good stead for the years ahead with children. You will understand how to read your dog and interpret his body language, a key factor in keeping children safe around dogs. You will have made practical preparations which will make the first exhausting weeks of parenthood just a little bit easier. And you will have some tactics to cope with the days when things aren't running smoothly.

One last important point to make is that the approach outlined in this book will serve you well for the years ahead. Babies develop rapidly physically and developmentally. From being a tiny infant, to rolling over, to sitting up, to grabbing, crawling and pulling themselves up seems to happen in the blink of an eye. Each of these stages will bring its own changes and challenges and it's important to be proactive in your approach as your baby grows. A dog that is relaxed about a newborn baby who doesn't really do very much may be more interested or concerned with a baby that is sitting up. A baby who has started to crawl may mean that your dog spends a little more time in a different room or behind a gate. It's important to remain aware of developmental changes and continue to adapt and adjust to account for them. Childhood is a series of stages and the principles you have learned in this book will help you tackle them with confidence.

My aim in writing this book is to help expectant parents feel confident and prepared for the weeks and months ahead and to help you avoid pitfalls which could potentially lead to stress for everyone in the family – human and canine. My hope is that the advice given in this book will help you make a smooth transition from dog parents to parents with a dog and help you get off to the best possible start to life as a family.

I wish you all the very best of luck in the wonderful adventure ahead.

APPENDIX A

TRAINING NOTES

The following training notes cover some very simple, foundation behaviours which are likely to be universally useful to all dog owners –

- Loose Lead Walking

- Focus Game

- Sit

- Positive Interrupter

- Go To Bed

- Crating Success

LOOSE LEAD WALKING

What is the goal?

To teach your dog to walk alongside you a slack lead

Why is this useful?

Being able to move in a comfortable connected manner makes walks more enjoyable for both ends of the lead. Loose lead walking protects your dog's neck from damage caused by pulling on his collar. It is safer for humans who might also be pushing a pram or walking with young children

How do we teach this?

- The following instructions are written for a dog walking on your left hand side. If you'd prefer your dog to walk on your right just reverse the instructions

- Start by facing your dog with a handful of food treats in your right fist (or in a treat pouch on your left whichever suits you best) and the lead hanging from your right wrist

- Keeping stationary, feed to your dog's mouth when they look at you. Repeat 3 times

- Now that you have their attention take one step backwards. If your dog moves to follow you, mark* the movement and feed your dog to his mouth with your left hand as he follows you

- Repeat until your dog is consistently following you as you move slowly backward

- You don't want to be walking backwards all your life so we are now going to transition to forward movement! After a few backward steps continue to move in the same direction but make a quarter turn to your right so that you are now walking sideways, or 'crabbing', with your dog on your left. Continue to mark* and feed to your dog's mouth as they move with you. If they surge forwards go back at the previous stage

- Continue until your dog is consistently following you as you move sideways

- Now, still moving in the same direction, make another quarter turn to your right so that you are now facing forward with your dog on your left. As they move with you mark* and feed them at your side. If you feed with your palm facing towards your dog this will help them stay in position and stop them moving round in front of you. If they begin to surge forward go back a stage

Tips

- start in a low distraction environment and gradually fade in distractions. If your dog begins to fail either go back a stage or reduce distractions

- keep sessions short and intersperse with some relaxed activity. Loose lead walking is hard for dogs and they won't be able to concentrate for long periods

- there is no "correct" side for your dog to walk on. Choose whichever side suits you both best

* "mark" means to use a click or a marker word (something short & clear like 'good', 'yes', 'nice') the instant the dog offers the behaviour you are looking for. This helps the dog learn exactly what behaviour is earning him a treat.

FOCUS GAME

What is the goal?

This simple but powerful game reinforces a default behaviour of standing calmly in front of a person with four paws on the floor offering calm attention.

Why is this useful?

This game helps settle your dog and focuses calm attention on you. Your dog learns a useful, baby compatible default behaviour of offering calm attention with four paws on the floor

How do we teach this?

- Start with 10 treats

- Letting the dog see the treat, toss one treat onto the floor between you and your dog

- Your dog will be likely to orient toward the food & eat it

- Say nothing and simply wait for your dog to look back towards you. Resist the urge to prompt or call your dog…we want him to re-engage on his own

- When he re-engages with you mark* that and then throw another piece of food out onto the floor

-

- Repeat for all 10 treats.

Tips

- Make sure you wait until your dog has looked back at you and you have marked the behaviour before you reach for the next treat. You want him looking at you to trigger you reaching for the treat not vice versa.

Changes in Criteria

- If at any time your dog is not re-engaging with you lower the criteria a little – drop the food closer to you or simply drop it at your feet, work in a lower distraction environment, use a higher value reward etc

- If your dog is doing well increase the criteria to strengthen and develop the behaviour – add in more distractions, work in lots of different places, change position (move slightly while the dog has oriented away from you, turn your body to face a slightly different direction etc), toss the food to the side or even behind you.

* "mark" means to use a click or a marker word (something short & clear like 'good', 'yes', 'nice') the

instant the dog offers the behaviour you are looking for. This helps the dog learn exactly what behaviour is earning him a treat.

SIT

What is the goal?

To teach your dog to sit in response to a cue

Why is this useful?

This behaviour can be useful for polite greetings as it keeps four feet on the floor so prevents jumping (But see below!)

How do we teach this?

- Hold a treat in your hand just in front of your dog's nose

- Slowly move your hand up and back over your dog's head

- Your dog will likely raise his head to follow the treat and as he does so his bottom will lower

- The instant the bottom starts to lower mark* that and then give your dog the treat by tossing it out to the side slightly (we want your dog to move out of position so that we can repeat the action. If he stays sitting we can't ask him to sit again!) At this stage you don't need the bottom to actually hit the floor. You can get there gradually over a few repetitions

- Once your pup is moving into a sit easily each time stop holding a treat in your hand and lure using an empty hand

- Add your cue word "sit" just before you start the hand movement

- Repeat, gradually making your hand movement smaller & smaller until you've faded it out completely and your dog is responding to your cue word alone.

Tips

- practice in different rooms, at different times of the day, in different positions (standing up, sitting in a chair, sitting on the floor etc)

- Have all the members of the family take part. You want your dog to listen to everyone...not just you!

A word of warning

Sit is very overused. There is no need to ask your dog to sit before dinner, sit at the kerb or sit to say hi. As long as your dog is standing calmly that's good enough. Sit isn't a natural or comfortable position for many dogs to do repeatedly or to hold for a long time so be mindful & thoughtful about when & why you're asking your dog to sit and don't overuse it.

* "mark" means to use a click or a marker word (something short & clear like 'good', 'yes', 'nice') the instant the dog offers the behaviour you are looking for. This helps the dog learn exactly what behaviour is earning him a treat.

POSITIVE INTERRUPTER

What is the goal?

To teach your dog a sound or phrase that enables you to interrupt what they are currently doing & orient immediately to you

Why is the useful?

Sometimes your dog will do things you don't want. Bark at the window, try to eat something disgusting from the ground...do dog stuff! A positive interrupter gives you a positive alternative to screaming "NO!" at them. It's used to interrupt unwanted behaviour giving you an opportunity to tell your dog what you would like him TO do instead.

How do we teach this?

- Pick a word, phrase or a sound. It can be anything at all. I tend to use "What's this?" or a kissy noise. Don't use their name as we overuse this and it doesn't often make an effective interrupter

- Grab some high value treats and start in a low distraction environment. Say your cue and then feed your dog a treat, whether he looks at you or not. Repeat until your dog is anticipating the arrival of the treat when he hears the cue

- Next, wait until your dog is looking away from you. Give your cue and as he turns towards you mark* that behaviour then give him a treat. At this stage I like to make the behaviour super rewarding but giving a few treats in a row, one after the other. Wait for your dog to disengage from you and then repeat. Keep sessions short (no more than 5 reps) but do them often

- As your dog responds reliably and quickly begin to add in distractions. Give your cue outside in the garden, out on a walk, when there are other dogs or people in the environment etc

- The key to this is repetition, repetition, repetition. But remember...little but often

- It's important to remember that this only interrupts a behaviour it doesn't tell your dog what you'd like him to do. So always follow up the interrupter with further information for your dog about what you'd like him TO do instead. For example, if he's heading toward the window to bark at the approaching postman, interrupt that, then call him to you & reinforce that alternative behaviour.

* "mark" means to use a click or a marker word (something short & clear like 'good', 'yes', 'nice') the

instant the dog offers the behaviour you are looking for. This helps the dog learn exactly what behaviour is earning him a treat.

GO TO BED

What is the goal?

To teach your dog to go to a mat/bed on cue & settle there.

Why is this useful?

Sometimes we need our dogs to settle quietly and/or settle in a place away from us. Teaching them what TO do when we are eating, working in the kitchen, answering the door, feeding the baby etc helps avoid unwanted behaviours.

How do we teach this?

I teach this using a really effective technique called backchaining. Back chaining involves teaching a skill starting with the endpoint and working back to the beginning. By teaching the last part first the learner is always moving toward the part of the skill that he learned first and with which he is most confident.

- Place the mat/bed on the floor in front of you.

- Lure your dog onto the mat and into a down position. Mark* and reward every few seconds while he remains lying down. Place the treat down on the mat between your dog's paws to encourage a downward focus. If he gets up simply lure him back into position and mark as soon as he lies down. Repeat for 20 repetitions to build a really strong association between lying on the mat & getting treats

- After you have done this for 20 or so repetitions begin to deliver the treat higher to bring your dog into a sit. Wait a moment and your dog is likely to move back into a down position since this behaviour has just been very strongly reinforced. When he moves into a down position, mark and treat, delivering the treat high to bring him into a sit. Repeat x 10

- Next time you mark your dog for moving into a down position, mark and deliver the treat by tossing it away from the mat. Because of the strong history you have just built of treats being delivered on the mat your dog is likely to return to the mat & lie down. Mark the instant they lie down & deliver the treat off the mat. Repeat x 10

- Once your dog is reliably returning to the mat/bed and lying down begin to add your cue just as they finish eating the previous treat.

Tips

- To increase difficulty - Begin to add in distractions. Practice in a busier room. Change your body position – stand up, sit down, move a couple of steps, move further away from the bed etc.

- To decrease difficulty - Minimise distractions and increase the rate of reinforcement. Keep training sessions short

- When teaching this at first it helps to always use the same bed or mat. Once your dog knows the behaviour he will be able to transfer the skill to different mats/beds

* "mark" means to use a click or a marker word (something short & clear like 'good', 'yes', 'nice') the instant the dog offers the behaviour you are looking for. This helps the dog learn exactly what behaviour is earning him a treat.

CRATING SUCCESS

If introduced sensitively and used appropriately crates offer a number of advantages both to you & to your dog. They become your dog's safe place. They are a secure way to separate your dog and your child when you need to. In the years to come they give your dog a breathing space away from a marauding toddler!

However there are come caveats –

- a crate should never be used as a punishment. It should have only good associations

- a crate should never be used for extended periods

Here are some simple ways to help your dog feel good about their crate.

Feeding

Feed your dog his meals in the crate to help create good associations with the crate. At first leave the door open while he eats and as he becomes more comfortable feed with the door closed.

Place tasty stuffed KONGs ™ in the crate. You can attach these to the crate using natural twine to encourage your dog to remain in the crate whilst he eats. Again, start with the door left open at first.

The Crate Fairy

Make good things magically appear in the crate for your dog to find! When your dog isn't looking pop something tasty into the crate - a piece of cheese or a slice of hot dog. Don't draw his attention to it....just let him find it himself . He'll begin to voluntarily check out his crate to see what has magically appeared.

Slowly, Slowly

The biggest mistake people make with crate training is going too fast.

Work at your dog's pace and increase criteria slowly & gently. Start with the crate door open. Toss a treat in as you say, "in you go". As soon as your dog eats the treat say, "out you come" and toss a treat outside the crate. Repeat until you have your dog moving into and out of the crate happily. Then begin moving the door a little when the dog is inside the crate – begin to close it a little more each time until you can close it completely, latch it & unlatch it , then open it again. From here we can begin to build a little duration by leaving the door shut for a little longer. Remember it's far better to go slowly and keep your dog happy & relaxed than push too far and create a bad association that has to be fixed later.

Not Just for Night Time

Some dogs are perfectly happy in their crate at night when the house is quiet but less happy being crated when things are going on elsewhere in the house. Use the crate at all times of the day to prevent it becoming associated only with night time. Start with brief periods in the crate while you are in the same room - while you make a cup of tea for example. Then build up to longer periods and begin to build in absences from the room too.

Movie Night

Another way to help your dog become used to being in the crate while you are around is to place the crate beside your chair and settle down to watch some television. Have a pot of treats beside you and every so often pop a treat in the crate. Again, this helps your dog get used to being in the crate whilst people are around while also building up duration spent in the crate.

Please Let Me In!

I love this one! It strengthens positive associations with the crate and gives you a dog who asks to be let into the crate! Place something awesome in the crate - a big piece of chicken or a generous chunk of hot dog. Then shut the door. Once your dog notices the food he will be keen to get access to the crate. You can then open the door and allow him to get the food.

APPENDIX B

ADDITIONAL RESOURCES

Websites

Family Paws Parent Education
(www.familypaws.com)

Doggone Safe (www.doggonsafe.com)

Stop the 77 (www.thefamilydog.com/stop-the-77)

Postpartum Support International
(www.postpartum.net)

Further Reading

Easy Peasy Doggy Squeezy, Steve Mann, 2020

Doggie Language: A Dog Lover's Guide to Understanding Your Best Friend, Lili Chin, 2020

Plenty in Life is Free: Reflections on Dogs, Training and Finding Grace, Kathy Sdao, 2012

Canine Enrichment: The Book Your Dog Wants You To Read, Shay Kelly, 2019

Facebook Groups

Dogs, Bumps & Babies

(www.facebook.com/groups/483666519040221/)

Beyond the Bowl – Canine Enrichment

(www.facebook.com/groups/1747279312231501)

Dog Training Advice & Support

(www.facebook.com/groups/374160792599484)

Products

KONG products (www.kongcompany.com)

Nina Ottoson (www.nina-ottosson.com)

K9 Connectables (www.k9connectables.com)

Lickimat (https://www.industripet.com/product-category/lickimats/)

Through a Dog's Ear (https://www.amazon.co.uk/Through-Dogs-Ear-Canine-Companion/dp/1591796423)

Sound Proof Puppy App

CONNECT WITH THE AUTHOR

I just wanted to take a moment to thank you so much for buying this book and, by doing so, helping to make the transition from dog parents to parents with a dog as stress free as possible for you and the much-loved dog(s) you share your life with. I hope you have enjoyed it and found the information helpful and now feel confident and ready for the next exciting chapter in your life.

Do you have any questions or feedback? I'd love to hear from you so please do get in touch.

You can connect with me on social media –

Facebook
www.facebook.com/theperfectpuppycompany

Instagram
www.instagram.com/theperfectpuppycompany

AND if you'd like to join my private Facebook community dedicated to positively raising dogs and children you would be very welcome. I share lots of valuable information on living with dogs and children and it's a safe and supportive group to share experiences and ask advice. Here's the link to join –

https://www.facebook.com/groups/483666519040221/

Or you can visit my website -

www.theperfectpuppycompany.co.uk

Or read and subscribe to my blog –

https://theperfectpuppycompany.wordpress.com

If you would like to work with me either in person in the Glasgow area, or remotely if you are further afield, then please contact me via my website -

https://www.theperfectpuppycompany.co.uk/contact-us

Printed in Great Britain
by Amazon